The Ultimate Plant Based Cookbook
for Beginners

1000-Day Plant-Based Recipes and 4-Week Meal Plan for Everyday

Delois Townsend

Table of Contents

Introduction 5
   What is a Plant-Based Diet 6
   How to Go Vegan? 6

Chapter 1: Breakfast Recipes 8
   Pumpkin Oatmeal 8
   Cauliflower Oatmeal 9
   Berry Cobbler 10
   Protein Bars 11
   Hemp Breakfast Cookies 12
   Strawberry Coconut Chia Pudding 13
   Zucchini Oatmeal 14
   Peanut Butter Muffins 15
   Chocolate Zucchini Bread 16
   Corn Muffins 17

Chapter 2: Smoothies Recipes 18
   Pumpkin Smoothie 18
   Banana Cream Chia Smoothie 19
   Mint Chocolate Smoothie 20
   Green Avocado Smoothie 21
   Green Apple Smoothie 22
   Chocolate Peanut Butter Smoothie 23
   Mango Lassi 24
   Pina Colada Smoothie 25

Chapter 3: Snack Recipes 26
   Spicy Almonds 26
   Roasted Chickpeas 27
   Kale Chips 28
   Carrot Chips 29
   Zucchini Chips 30
   Banana Chips 31
   Apple Leather 32
   Seeds Crackers 33

Chapter 4: Salads and Sides Recipes 34
   Chickpea Salad 34
   Cabbage Mango Slaw 35
   Quinoa Crunch Salad 36
   Fennel Salad with Cucumber 37
   Curry Tofu Salad 38
   Farro Tabbouleh Salad 39
   Kohlrabi Slaw with Cilantro 40
   Thai Noodle Salad 41

Chapter 5: Dips and Sauces Recipes 42
   Spinach Dip 42
   Ranch Dressing 43
   Buffalo Dip 44
   Broccoli Dip 45
   Roasted Cauliflower Dip 46
   Eggplant Dip 47

Chapter 6: Lunch Recipes ... 48

Coconut Green Soup ... 48

Roasted Cauliflower Soup ... 50

Squash and Chestnut Soup ... 51

Shiitake Tortilla Soup ... 52

Vegan Tomato Soup ... 53

Pita Pizzas ... 54

Black Bean Burgers ... 55

Spinach-Potato Tacos ... 56

Sweet Potato Quesadillas ... 57

Slow-Cooker Chili ... 58

Sweet Potato Chili with Kale ... 59

Potato-Cauliflower Curry ... 60

Zucchini and Chickpea Sauté ... 61

Raw Collard Wraps ... 62

Avocado Chickpea Lettuce Cups ... 63

Chapter 7: Dinner Recipes ... 64

Lime Bean Artichoke Wraps ... 64

Butternut Squash Lasagna ... 65

Sweet Potato Penne Pasta ... 67

Roasted Butternut Squash Pasta ... 68

Cashew Mac and Cheese ... 69

Taco Pasta with Sweet Corn ... 70

Vegetarian Lentil Loaf ... 71

Black Bean Loaf with Avocado Sauce ... 73

Pineapple Tofu Kabobs ... 74

Lentil Sloppy Joes with Spaghetti Squash ... 75

Sesame-Orange Chickpea Stir-Fry ... 76

Sweet Potato Zoodles ... 77

Butternut Squash Chickpea Stew ... 78

Puerto Rican Rice and Beans ... 79

Curried Brown Rice with Tofu ... 81

Chapter 8: Desserts Recipes ... 83

Cashew Oat Muffins ... 83

Banana Walnut Muffins ... 84

Protein Fat Bombs ... 85

Apple Pie Bites ... 86

Peach Popsicles ... 87

Green Popsicles ... 88

Strawberry Coconut Popsicles ... 89

Crunchy Chocolate Brownies ... 90

Chickpea Meringues ... 91

Watermelon Coconut Sorbet ... 92

Chapter 9: 30-Day Meal Plan ... 93

Week 1 ... 93

Week 2 ... 94

Week 3 ... 95

Week 4 ... 96

Conclusion ... 97

Introduction

Introducing a healthy diet into today's lifestyle is never easy, yet it is also equally important. To live a productive and active life, we all need to maintain a positive relationship with the food we eat. And a healthy diet can help to make better choices and develop good eating habits. Though there are several promising diet plans that are available today the ones that practically ensure good health are rare to find. The plant-based diet is one such approach that is known for improving health. The diet makes a clear distinction between what to eat and what not to, but since we are living in the age of processed food products, the line between the two often gets blurred. So, the purpose of this cookbook is to clear your mind and bust all the confusion out of your mind regarding the plant-based diet with all the easy-to-follow plant-based recipes and a 30 days' meal plan to get started with.

What is a Plant-Based Diet

The plant-based diet is restrictive, and it prohibits the use of animal-sourced food while promoting the use of plant-based food items. For these two reasons, the diet has been known to provide lots of health benefits. By removing the animal-sourced products, a lot of saturated fats are also removed from the diet. And by introducing plant-based products, a dieter introduces more of the antioxidants into the diet, which helps improve the health in many ways.

1. It can reduce the risks of heart diseases, especially Heart Stroke.
2. It can promote a healthy body weight.
3. It can help protect against certain cancers due to the phytonutrients present in a plant-based diet.
4. It can help control high blood pressure due to the healthy fat content.
5. It can help prevent high cholesterol levels as plant-based products have lesser cholesterols than animal-sourced products.

How to Go Vegan?

If you are planning to live on a plant-based diet, here are things that you can frequently add to your routine meals. Try to stuff your refrigerators with all the relevant ingredients and keep yourself safe from any distractions.

Food for Plant-Based Diet

Following is the list of the food that you can freely consume on a plant-based diet:

1. Vegan Meat:

You can have more proteins on the menu without having any meat, poultry, and seafood by adding the following items to the meals:

- Tofu
- Tempeh
- Seitan
- Vegan cheese (made out of tofu)
- Soba noodles

2. Fruits

Fruits are a great source of good energy, filled with lots of vitamins, fibers, and minerals. If you are looking for some clean carbs, then all the fruits are great to have on this diet.

3. Vegetables

Without vegetables, the plant-based is incomplete. The more vegetables you add to your platter, the better and more nutritious your meal gets. Juicy and rich vegetables also add good flavors and lots of calories to the menu. You can add them to soups, stews, pasta, breakfast, snacks, or smoothies.

4. Legumes

Legumes can be consumed on this diet to meet all the protein needs. Try to add all the varieties of beans, lentils, and chickpeas to your plant-based menu:

- chickpeas
- lentils
- peas
- black beans

Introduction

Introducing a healthy diet into today's lifestyle is never easy, yet it is also equally important. To live a productive and active life, we all need to maintain a positive relationship with the food we eat. And a healthy diet can help to make better choices and develop good eating habits. Though there are several promising diet plans that are available today the ones that practically ensure good health are rare to find. The plant-based diet is one such approach that is known for improving health. The diet makes a clear distinction between what to eat and what not to, but since we are living in the age of processed food products, the line between the two often gets blurred. So, the purpose of this cookbook is to clear your mind and bust all the confusion out of your mind regarding the plant-based diet with all the easy-to-follow plant-based recipes and a 30 days' meal plan to get started with.

What is a Plant-Based Diet

The plant-based diet is restrictive, and it prohibits the use of animal-sourced food while promoting the use of plant-based food items. For these two reasons, the diet has been known to provide lots of health benefits. By removing the animal-sourced products, a lot of saturated fats are also removed from the diet. And by introducing plant-based products, a dieter introduces more of the antioxidants into the diet, which helps improve the health in many ways.

1. It can reduce the risks of heart diseases, especially Heart Stroke.
2. It can promote a healthy body weight.
3. It can help protect against certain cancers due to the phytonutrients present in a plant-based diet.
4. It can help control high blood pressure due to the healthy fat content.
5. It can help prevent high cholesterol levels as plant-based products have lesser cholesterols than animal-sourced products.

How to Go Vegan?

If you are planning to live on a plant-based diet, here are things that you can frequently add to your routine meals. Try to stuff your refrigerators with all the relevant ingredients and keep yourself safe from any distractions.

Food for Plant-Based Diet

Following is the list of the food that you can freely consume on a plant-based diet:

1. Vegan Meat:

You can have more proteins on the menu without having any meat, poultry, and seafood by adding the following items to the meals:

- Tofu
- Tempeh
- Seitan
- Vegan cheese (made out of tofu)
- Soba noodles

2. Fruits

Fruits are a great source of good energy, filled with lots of vitamins, fibers, and minerals. If you are looking for some clean carbs, then all the fruits are great to have on this diet.

3. Vegetables

Without vegetables, the plant-based is incomplete. The more vegetables you add to your platter, the better and more nutritious your meal gets. Juicy and rich vegetables also add good flavors and lots of calories to the menu. You can add them to soups, stews, pasta, breakfast, snacks, or smoothies.

4. Legumes

Legumes can be consumed on this diet to meet all the protein needs. Try to add all the varieties of beans, lentils, and chickpeas to your plant-based menu:

- chickpeas
- lentils
- peas
- black beans

- kidney beans

5. Seeds and Nuts:

A drizzle of nuts and seeds on top of salads and desserts can increase their nutritional values up too many folds.

6. Healthy Fats

Almost all the plant-sourced oils and fats are unsaturated and low in cholesterol. There is a wide variety of plant-based oils that you can use:

- walnut oil
- Sesame oil
- avocado oil
- chia seed oil etc.

7. Whole Grains

Whole grains also make another important group of plant-based diet food as they are a rich source of energy:

- quinoa
- oat
- brown rice
- spelt
- buckwheat
- wholegrain bread
- rye
- barley

8. Plant-based Milk and Dairy:

As animal-based milk and other dairy products are not allowed on a plant-based diet, there is another plant-based substitute that you can frequently consume. The plant-based milk and dairy that are sourced from different nuts have good taste and texture. They are also low on carbs.

- almond milk
- coconut milk
- coconut cream
- cashew milk
- cashew cream
- cashew yogurt
- soy milk
- rice milk
- oat milk
- hemp milk

Foods to Avoid

A plant-based diet omits all the animal source meals from the menu and provides us a wide variety of vegan options. Based on their source and nutritional content, following animal-sourced food items are strictly prohibited on the plant-based diet.

- All animal fats, including butter, ghee.
- Animal meat: seafood, lamb, poultry, pork, and beef.
- Dairy products like milk, eggs, cream, yogurt, cheese, cream cheese.
- Sugary market foods items: biscuits, cakes, and pastries that contain eggs and milk.
- All processed food products with animal-sourced ingredients.

Chapter 1: Breakfast Recipes

Pumpkin Oatmeal

Prep Time: 15 minutes.

Cook Time: 45 minutes.

Serves: 4

Ingredients:

- 2½ cups rolled oats
- 3 tablespoons chia seeds
- 1 teaspoon baking powder
- 1 teaspoon cinnamon
- ½ teaspoon cardamom
- ½ teaspoon salt
- 1¾ cups almond milk
- 1 (15-ounce) can pumpkin
- ⅓ cup maple syrup
- 1 tablespoon pure vanilla extract

Preparation:

1. Preheat your oven to 350°F.
2. Layer an 8x8-inch baking dish with wax paper.
3. Mix oats with salt, cardamom, cinnamon, baking powder, and chia seeds in a bowl.
4. Now, stir the rest of the oatmeal ingredients and mix it well until smooth.
5. Spread this batter in the baking dish and bake for 45 minutes.
6. Allow the oatmeal to cool and serve.

Serving Suggestion: Serve the oatmeal with a glass of green smoothie.

Variation Tip: Drizzle roasted pumpkin seeds over the oatmeal.

Nutritional Information Per Serving:

Calories 284 | Fat 7.9g |Sodium 704mg | Carbs 31g | Fiber 3.6g | Sugar 6g | Protein 8g

Cauliflower Oatmeal

Prep Time: 15 minutes.
Cook Time: 15 minutes.
Serves: 2

Ingredients:

- 1 cup cauliflower rice
- ½ cup unsweetened almond milk
- ½ teaspoon cinnamon
- 1 tablespoon honey
- ½ tablespoon peanut butter
- 1 strawberry, sliced

Preparation:

1. Mix milk with cauliflower rice, honey and cinnamon in a saucepan.
2. Cook the rice mixture to a boil then reduce the heat to low.
3. Now cook the mixture for 10 minutes on a simmer.
4. Allow the oatmeal to cool, then garnish it with a strawberry.
5. Serve.

Serving Suggestion: Serve the oatmeal with a glass of avocado smoothie.

Variation Tip: Add more berries to the oatmeal.

Nutritional Information Per Serving:

Calories 234 | Fat 4.7g |Sodium 1mg | Carbs 18g | Fiber 7g | Sugar 3.3g | Protein 6g

Berry Cobbler

Prep Time: 15 minutes.
Cook Time: 30 minutes.
Serves: 4

Ingredients:

- 1 cup fresh blueberries
- 1 cup fresh blackberries
- 1 cup fresh raspberries
- 1 cup of water
- 3 tablespoons tapioca starch
- ½ teaspoon cinnamon
- ¼ cup coconut sugar
- Cobbler topping
- 1 cup rolled oats
- ⅔ cup whole wheat flour
- ¼ cup coconut sugar
- 1 tablespoon flaxseeds
- 1 tablespoon hemp seeds
- 1 tablespoon chia seeds
- 3 tablespoons coconut oil, melted
- ⅓ cup almond milk
- ¼ teaspoon pure vanilla extract
- ¼ teaspoon cinnamon
- ¾ teaspoon baking powder
- 1 pinch of pink salt

Preparation:

1. Preheat your oven to 375°F.
2. Mix all the berries filling ingredients in a saucepan and cook on a simmer until it thickens.
3. Remove the filling from the heat and spread it in a greased baking dish.
4. Mix oats with coconut sugar with cinnamon, hemp shells, chia seeds, flour, flaxseeds, salt and baking powder in a large bowl.
5. Stir in vanilla, milk and coconut oil, then mix well.
6. Spread this batter on top of the filling.
7. Bake the cobbler for 30 minutes at 375°F
8. Allow it to cool and serve.

Serving Suggestion: Serve the cobbler with a glass of blueberry smoothie.

Variation Tip: Replace blueberries with strawberries for change of taste.

Nutritional Information Per Serving:

Calories 317 | Fat 13g | Sodium 114mg | Carbs 31g | Fiber 1g | Sugar 10g | Protein 11g

Protein Bars

Prep Time: 10 minutes.
Cook Time: 20 minutes.
Serves: 6

Ingredients:

- 1½ cup quick-cooking oats
- ½ cup almond meal
- ½ cup flaxseed meal
- 2 teaspoons cinnamon
- ½ teaspoon salt
- 4 tablespoons vegan protein powder
- 1 teaspoon pure vanilla extract
- 2 bananas, ripe and mashed
- ½ cup applesauce
- ¼ cup creamy peanut butter
- 2 tablespoons honey

Preparation:

1. Preheat your oven to 350℉ .
2. Layer an 8x8 square baking dish with cooking spray.
3. Mix all the ingredients in a large bowl.
4. Spread this mixture in the prepared pan.
5. Bake the batter for 20 minutes in the oven.
6. Allow the mixture to cool, then slice.
7. Serve.

Serving Suggestion: Serve the bars with a glass of peanut butter smoothie.

Variation Tip: Drizzle chocolate syrup over the bars.

Nutritional Information Per Serving:

Calories 248 | Fat 12g |Sodium 321mg | Carbs 26g | Fiber 4g | Sugar 8g | Protein 7g

Hemp Breakfast Cookies

Prep Time: 10 minutes.
Cook Time: 15 minutes.
Serves: 6

Ingredients:

- 3 cups almond flour
- 1 cup dried dates, pitted
- ½ cup hemp seeds
- 1 cup almond milk

Preparation:

1. Mix almond milk with hemp seeds and dates in a bowl and leave for 1 hour.
2. Blend almond flour with the rest of the ingredients and milk mixture in a mixer until it makes a smooth dough.
3. Preheat your oven to 350°F.
4. Divide the dough into 9 portions and shape each into a cookie.
5. Place these cookies in a baking sheet, lined with wax paper.
6. Bake the cookies for 15 minutes in the oven and flip them once cooked halfway through.
7. Serve.

Serving Suggestion: Serve the cookies with a glass of blueberry smoothie.

Variation Tip: Drizzle chocolate syrup over the cookies.

Nutritional Information Per Serving:

Calories 217 | Fat 25g |Sodium 132mg | Carbs 29g | Fiber 3.9g | Sugar 3g | Protein 8.9g

Strawberry Coconut Chia Pudding

Prep Time: 15 minutes.

Cook Time: 0 minutes.

Serves: 2

Ingredients:

- 2 tablespoons chia seeds
- 1 cup of canned coconut milk
- ¼ cup strawberries, chopped
- ½ teaspoon vanilla extract
- ½ teaspoon stevia

Preparation:

1. Add strawberries and all the ingredients to a mason jar.
2. Cover its lid and refrigerate overnight.
3. Serve.

Serving Suggestion: Serve the pudding with a glass of blueberry smoothie.

Variation Tip: Drizzle shaved chocolate over the pudding.

Nutritional Information Per Serving:

Calories 311 | Fat 12.5g | Sodium 595mg | Carbs 13g | Fiber 12g | Sugar 12g | Protein 7g

Zucchini Oatmeal

Prep Time: 15 minutes.
Cook Time: 4 minutes.
Serves: 4

Ingredients:

- 2 cups rolled oats
- 6 tablespoons pea protein
- 2 teaspoons cinnamon
- 1 teaspoon nutmeg
- 2 ¼ cups almond milk
- 1 cup zucchini, grated
- ¼ cup maple syrup
- 1 teaspoon vanilla extract
- Toppings
- Banana
- Nuts
- Seeds
- Sugar-free chocolate chips
- 1 teaspoon coconut oil, melted

Preparation:

1. Sauté oats with coconut oil in an Instant Pot for 2 minutes on Sauté mode.
2. Stir in the rest of the ingredients, cover and seal its lid.
3. Cook for 2 minutes on high pressure.
4. When done, release all the pressure and remove the lid.
5. Allow the oatmeal to cool and garnish with desired toppings.
6. Serve.

Serving Suggestion: Serve the oatmeal with a glass of pumpkin smoothie.

Variation Tip: Drizzle chocolate syrup over the oatmeal.

Nutritional Information Per Serving:

Calories 232 | Fat 12g |Sodium 202mg | Carbs 26g | Fiber 4g | Sugar 8g | Protein 7.3g

Peanut Butter Muffins

Prep Time: 15 minutes.

Cook Time: 27 minutes.

Serves: 6

Ingredients:

- ¾ cup oat flour
- ¼ cup coconut sugar
- 2 tablespoons pea protein powder
- 1 tablespoon baking powder
- 2 teaspoons baking soda
- 3 large bananas, mashed
- ½ cup peanut butter
- 2 tablespoons flaxseed
- ½ cup water
- ½ cup almond milk
- 1 teaspoon vanilla extract

Preparation:

1. Preheat the oven to 350°F and layer two muffin trays with cupcake liners.
2. Soak flaxseed with ½ cup water in a bowl for 5 minutes.
3. Mix mashed banana with milk, peanut butter and flaxseed mixture in a large bowl.
4. Now, stir it with the rest of the muffin ingredients and mix well evenly.
5. Divide the prepared batter into the muffin tray and bake for 27 minutes.
6. Allow the muffins to cool and serve.

Serving Suggestion: Serve the muffins with a glass of blueberry smoothie.

Variation Tip: Drizzle chocolate syrup over the muffins.

Nutritional Information Per Serving:

Calories 297 | Fat 15g |Sodium 548mg | Carbs 35g | Fiber 4g | Sugar 1g | Protein 9g

Chocolate Zucchini Bread

Prep Time: 15 minutes.
Cook Time: 55 minutes.
Serves: 6

Ingredients:

- 1¼ cup whole wheat flour
- ¾ cup coconut sugar
- ½ cup raw cacao powder
- 3 teaspoons baking powder
- 2 teaspoons baking soda
- 1 cup zucchini, shredded
- ½ cup almond milk
- ⅓ cup unsweetened applesauce
- ⅓ cup coconut oil, melted
- 2 teaspoons vanilla extract
- ⅔ cup sugar-free chocolate chip

Preparation:

1. Preheat your oven to 350°F and layer a 9-inch loaf pan with wax paper.
2. Pat dry the shredded zucchini and keep it aside.
3. Mix flour with baking soda, baking powder, cacao powder, coconut sugar and flour in a bowl.
4. Stir it with vanilla, applesauce, milk, and peanut butter, then mix until smooth.
5. Fold in sugar-free chocolate chips and zucchini shreds.
6. Spread this batter in the prepared loaf pan.
7. Bake this bread for 55 minutes in the oven.
8. Allow the bread to cool, then slice.
9. Serve.

Serving Suggestion: Serve the bread with a glass of strawberry smoothie.

Variation Tip: Drizzle chocolate syrup over the bread.

Nutritional Information Per Serving:

Calories 218 | Fat 22g |Sodium 350mg | Carbs 22g | Fiber 0.7g | Sugar 1g | Protein 2.3g

Corn Muffins

Prep Time: 15 minutes.
Cook Time: 20 minutes.
Serves: 6

Ingredients:

- 1½ tablespoons ground flaxseed
- 1 cup almond milk
- ½ cup applesauce
- ½ cup pure maple syrup
- 1 cup corn meal
- 1 cup oat flour
- 1 teaspoon baking soda
- 1 teaspoon baking powder
- ½ teaspoon salt
- 1 cup corn kernels

Preparation:

1. Preheat your oven to 375°F.
2. Mix almond milk with flaxseed in a large bowl then leave it for 5 minutes.
3. Stir it in maple syrup and apple sauce then mix well.
4. Add salt, baking powder, baking soda, oat flour and cornmeal then mix until smooth.
5. Add corn kernels and mix evenly.
6. Divide the corn batter into 12 muffin cups and bake for 20 minutes in the oven.
7. Allow the muffins to cool and serve.

Serving Suggestion: Serve the muffins with a glass of blueberry smoothie.

Variation Tip: Drizzle chocolate syrup over the muffins.

Nutritional Information Per Serving:

Calories 257 | Fat 12g | Sodium 48mg | Carbs 32g | Fiber 2g | Sugar 0g | Protein 14g

Chapter 2: Smoothies Recipes

Pumpkin Smoothie

Prep Time: 5 minutes.
Cook Time: 0 minutes.
Serves: 2

Ingredients:

- 1 banana frozen
- ½ cup pumpkin puree
- 1 cup almond milk
- ½ teaspoon pumpkin pie spice
- 1 tablespoon maple syrup
- ½ cup ice cubes

Preparation:

1. Blend banana, pumpkin puree, milk, maple, ice and pumpkin spice in a blender until smooth.
2. Serve chilled.

Serving Suggestion: Serve the smoothie with your favorite muffins.

Variation Tip: Add chopped nuts to the smoothie.

Nutritional Information Per Serving:

Calories 204 | Fat 13g | Sodium 216mg | Carbs 17g | Fiber 3g | Sugar 4g | Protein 3g

Banana Cream Chia Smoothie

Prep Time: 5 minutes.

Cook Time: 0 minutes.

Serves: 1

Ingredients:

- ¼ cup chia seeds
- ½ cup full-fat coconut milk
- ½ cup almond milk
- 1 tablespoon agave syrup
- 1 teaspoon cinnamon
- 1 banana, mashed

Preparation:

1. Blend banana mash with milk, agave and cinnamon in a blender.
2. Stir it in chia seeds and leave for 15 minutes.
3. Serve chilled.

Serving Suggestion: Serve the smoothie with your favorite muffins.

Variation Tip: Add shredded coconut to the smoothie.

Nutritional Information Per Serving:

Calories 380 | Fat 19g |Sodium 318mg | Carbs 19g | Fiber 5g | Sugar 3g | Protein 6g

Mint Chocolate Smoothie

Prep Time: 5 minutes.

Cook Time: 0 minutes.

Serves: 1

Ingredients:

- 1 scoop vegan protein powder
- 1 tablespoon ground flaxseed
- 1 medium banana
- 1 cup fresh spinach
- ¼ teaspoon peppermint extract
- 4 ice cubes
- ¾ cup almond milk
- 1 tablespoon coconut nectar
- 1 tablespoon dark chocolate, chopped

Preparation:

1. Blend protein powder, banana and rest of the ingredients in a blender until smooth.
2. Serve chilled.

Serving Suggestion: Serve the smoothie with your favorite muffins.

Variation Tip: Add chopped nuts to the smoothie.

Nutritional Information Per Serving:

Calories 273 | Fat 8g | Sodium 146mg | Carbs 18g | Fiber 5g | Sugar 1g | Protein 2g

Green Avocado Smoothie

Prep Time: 5 minutes.

Cook Time: 0 minutes.

Serves: 1

Ingredients:

- 1 banana
- ½ avocado
- 1 cup baby spinach
- ½ cup coconut yogurt
- ½ lemon, juiced
- 1 cup water

Preparation:

1. Blend avocado, banana and rest of the ingredients in a blender until smooth.
2. Serve chilled.

Serving Suggestion: Serve the smoothie with your favorite muffins.

Variation Tip: Add chopped apples to the smoothie.

Nutritional Information Per Serving:

Calories 240 | Fat 5g | Sodium 244mg | Carbs 26g | Fiber 1g | Sugar 1g | Protein 27g

Green Apple Smoothie

Prep Time: 5 minutes.
Cook Time: 0 minutes.
Serves: 2

Ingredients:

- 1 large green apple
- 4 Medjool dates
- 3 cups spinach
- 8 ice cubes
- ½ cup water
- 1 teaspoon lemon juice

Preparation:

1. Blend apple, dates and rest of the ingredients in a blender until smooth.
2. Serve chilled.

Serving Suggestion: Serve the smoothie with your favorite muffins.

Variation Tip: Add chopped peaches to the smoothie.

Nutritional Information Per Serving:

Calories 282 | Fat 4g |Sodium 232mg | Carbs 24g | Fiber 1g | Sugar 0g | Protein 11g

Chocolate Peanut Butter Smoothie

Prep Time: 5 minutes.

Cook Time: 0 minutes.

Serves: 1

Ingredients:

- 2 frozen bananas
- 3 tablespoons cacao powder
- 3 tablespoons peanut butter
- 1 cup almond milk

Preparation:

1. Blend peanut butter, bananas and rest of the ingredients in a blender until smooth.
2. Serve chilled.

Serving Suggestion: Serve the peanut butter smoothie with your favorite muffins.

Variation Tip: Add shredded coconut to the smoothie.

Nutritional Information Per Serving:

Calories 329 | Fat 5g |Sodium 510mg | Carbs 37g | Fiber 5g | Sugar 4g | Protein 1g

Mango Lassi

Prep Time: 5 minutes.
Cook Time: 0 minutes.
Serves: 2

Ingredients:

- 1 cup soy yogurt
- 1 cup frozen mango chunks
- ¼ cup soy milk
- 2 Medjool dates, pitted

Preparation:

1. Blend soy yogurt with mango, milk and dates in a blender until smooth.
2. Serve.

Serving Suggestion: Serve the mango lassi with your favorite muffins.

Variation Tip: Add chopped mangos on top of the smoothie.

Nutritional Information Per Serving:

Calories 201 | Fat 7g |Sodium 269mg | Carbs 25g | Fiber 4g | Sugar 12g | Protein 2g

Pina Colada Smoothie

Prep Time: 5 minutes.

Cook Time: 0 minutes.

Serves: 2

Ingredients:

- ½ cup Malibu coconut rum
- 2 cups fresh pineapple juice
- 1 cup coconut cream
- 1 cup ice
- 2 tablespoons coconut sugar

Preparation:

1. Blend pineapple juice and the rest of the ingredients in a blender jug until creamy.
2. Pour into glasses and garnish with pineapple.
3. Serve.

Serving Suggestion: Serve the pina colada with your favorite muffins.

Variation Tip: Add chopped nuts or shredded coconut to the smoothie.

Nutritional Information Per Serving:

Calories 348 | Fat 12g | Sodium 710mg | Carbs 24g | Fiber 5g | Sugar 3g | Protein 3g

Chapter 3: Snack Recipes

Spicy Almonds

Prep Time: 15 minutes.
Cook Time: 10 minutes.
Serves: 4

Ingredients:

- 2 cups whole almonds
- 1 tablespoon chili powder
- ½ teaspoon ground cinnamon
- ½ teaspoon ground cumin
- ½ teaspoon ground coriander
- Salt and black pepper, to taste
- 1 tablespoon olive oil

Preparation:

1. Preheat your oven to 375°F.
2. Line a suitable baking pan with parchment paper.
3. Toss almonds with all the spices and oil.
4. Spread the almond mixture into the prepared baking dish in a single layer.
5. Roast for about 10 minutes, flipping twice.
6. Remove from the oven and let it cool completely before serving.

Serving Suggestion: Serve the peanuts with sautéed peas snaps.

Variation Tip: Add some smoked paprika for seasoning.

Nutritional Information Per Serving:

Calories 175 | Fat 16g | Sodium 255mg | Carbs 21g | Fiber 1.2g | Sugar 5g | Protein 2.1g

Roasted Chickpeas

Prep Time: 15 minutes.
Cook Time: 30 minutes.
Serves: 4

Ingredients:

- ¾ cup tamarind purée
- 2 cups canned chickpeas, rinsed and drained
- 1 tablespoon olive oil
- 1 teaspoon dried marjoram, crushed
- 1 teaspoon ground cumin
- ½ teaspoon cayenne pepper
- ¼ teaspoon ground allspice
- Salt, to taste

Preparation:

1. Preheat your oven to 450°F.
2. Arrange a rack in the upper third of the oven.
3. With paper towels, pat dry the chickpeas.
4. In a bowl, add the chickpeas and remaining ingredients and toss to coat well.
5. Spread the chickpeas onto a rimmed baking sheet.
6. Bake for about 25-30 minutes, stirring once halfway through.
7. Serve.

Serving Suggestion: Serve the chickpeas with a glass of orange juice on the side

Variation Tip: Add lemon juice for a refreshing taste.

Nutritional Information Per Serving:

Calories 135 | Fat 25g | Sodium 122mg | Carbs 33g | Fiber 0.4g | Sugar 1g | Protein 3g

Kale Chips

Prep Time: 10 minutes.

Cook Time: 15 minutes.

Serves: 4

Ingredients:

- 1-pound fresh kale leaves stemmed and torn
- ¼ teaspoon cayenne pepper
- Salt, to taste
- 1 tablespoon olive oil

Preparation:

1. Preheat your oven to 350°F.
2. Line a suitable baking sheet with parchment paper.
3. Arrange the kale pieces onto the prepared baking sheet in a single layer.
4. Sprinkle the kale with cayenne pepper and salt and drizzle with oil.
5. Bake for about 10-15 minutes then allow them to cool.
6. Serve.

Serving Suggestion: Serve the kale chips with vegan cheese dip.

Variation Tip: Add paprika to season the chips.

Nutritional Information Per Serving:

Calories 129 | Fat 17g |Sodium 422mg | Carbs 5g | Fiber 0g | Sugar 1g | Protein 4g

Carrot Chips

Prep Time: 15 minutes.
Cook Time: 30 minutes.
Serves: 4

Ingredients:

- 2 medium carrots, peeled and sliced thinly
- 1 tablespoon canola oil
- Salt, to taste

Preparation:

1. Preheat your oven to 350°F.
2. Line 2 suitable baking sheets with parchment paper.
3. In a large bowl, add the carrot slices and oil and toss to coat well.
4. Arrange the carrot slices onto the prepared baking sheets in a single layer.
5. Bake for about 20-30 minutes then allow them to cool.
6. Serve

Serving Suggestion: Serve the carrot chips with tomato sauce.

Variation Tip: Add paprika to season the chips.

Nutritional Information Per Serving:

Calories 184 | Fat 2g | Sodium 460mg | Carbs 6g | Fiber 0.4g | Sugar 2g | Protein 2g

Zucchini Chips

Prep Time: 10 minutes.
Cook Time: 15 minutes.
Serves: 2

Ingredients:

- 1 medium zucchini, cut into thin slices
- ⅛ teaspoon ground turmeric
- ⅛ teaspoon ground cumin
- Salt, to taste
- 2 teaspoons olive oil

Preparation:

1. Preheat your oven to 400°F.
2. Line 2 baking sheets with parchment papers.
3. Toss zucchini slices with spices and oil in a bowl.
4. Transfer the zucchini mixture onto the prepared baking sheets in a single layer.
5. Bake for about 10-15 minutes.
6. Serve immediately.

Serving Suggestion: Serve the zucchini chips with tomato sauce.

Variation Tip: Add paprika to season the chips.

Nutritional Information Per Serving:

Calories 152 | Fat 2.4g | Sodium 216mg | Carbs 6g | Fiber 2.3g | Sugar 1.2g | Protein 7g

Banana Chips

Prep Time: 15 minutes.

Cook Time: 60 minutes.

Serves: 2

Ingredients:

- 2 large bananas, peeled and cut into ¼-inch thick slices
- ½ teaspoon ground cinnamon

Preparation:

1. Preheat your oven to 250°F.
2. Line a suitable baking sheet with parchment paper.
3. Place the banana slices onto a prepared baking sheet.
4. Bake for about 1 hour.
5. Remove the banana chips from the oven and set aside to cool.
6. Serve.

Serving Suggestion: Serve the banana chips with chocolate sauce.

Variation Tip: You can also coat the banana with cinnamon-sugar mixture.

Nutritional Information Per Serving:

Calories 288 | Fat 8g | Sodium 611mg | Carbs 18g | Fiber 0g | Sugar 4g | Protein 13g

Apple Leather

Prep Time: 15 minutes.
Cook Time: 15 minutes.
Serves: 8

Ingredients:

- 1 cup water
- 8 cups apples, peeled, cored and chopped
- 1 tablespoon ground cinnamon
- 2 tablespoons fresh lemon juice

Preparation:

1. In a large pan, add water and apples over medium-low heat and simmer for about 10-15 minutes, stirring occasionally.
2. Remove from heat and set aside to cool slightly.
3. In a blender, add apple mixture and pulse until smooth.
4. Return the mixture into the pan over medium-low heat.
5. Stir in cinnamon and lemon juice and simmer for about 10 minutes.
6. Transfer the mixture onto dehydrator trays and, with the back of the spoon, smooth the top.
7. Set the dehydrator at 135°F.
8. Dehydrate for about 10-12 hours.
9. Cut the apple leather into equal-sized rectangles.
10. Now, roll each rectangle to make fruit rolls.

Serving Suggestion: Serve the apple leather with a bowl of fresh berries.

Variation Tip: Add a small drop of vanilla essence.

Nutritional Information Per Serving:

Calories 201 | Fat 16g |Sodium 412mg | Carbs 24g | Fiber 0.2g | Sugar 1g | Protein 8.2g

Seeds Crackers

Prep Time: 15 minutes.
Cook Time: 35 minutes.
Serves: 6

Ingredients:

- 3 tablespoons water
- 1 tablespoon chia seeds
- 3 tablespoons sunflower seeds
- 1 tablespoon quinoa flour
- 1 teaspoon ground turmeric
- Pinch of ground cinnamon
- Salt, to taste

Preparation:

1. Preheat your oven to 345°F. Line a baking sheet with parchment paper.
2. In a bowl, add the water and chia seeds and set aside for about 15 minutes.
3. Then add the remaining ingredients and mix well.
4. Spread the mixture onto the prepared baking sheet evenly.
5. Bake for about 20 minutes.
6. Remove from the oven and place onto a wire rack to cool completely before serving.
7. Break into pieces and serve.

Serving Suggestion: Serve the crackers with your favorite vegan dip.

Variation Tip: Season the crackers with some dried herbs.

Nutritional Information Per Serving:

Calories 231 | Fat 20.1g |Sodium 364mg | Carbs 13g | Fiber 1g | Sugar 1.4g | Protein 5g

Chapter 4: Salads and Sides Recipes

Chickpea Salad

Prep Time: 10 minutes.
Cook Time: 0 minutes.
Serves: 6

Ingredients:

- 3 cups cooked garbanzo beans
- 1 red bell pepper, diced
- 1 yellow bell pepper, diced
- 1 cup vine tomatoes, chopped
- 1 cup cucumber, chopped
- 5 scallions, sliced
- 1 cup fresh mint, chopped
- 1 cup Italian parsley, chopped
- 1 garlic clove, minced
- Salt and black pepper, to taste
- ½ cup olive oil
- Zest of 1 lemon
- ¼ cup lemon juice
- 1 teaspoon sumac
- ½ teaspoon cayenne chili flakes

Preparation:

1. Mix beans with bell pepper, cucumber and the rest of the ingredients in a salad bowl.
2. Serve.

Serving Suggestion: Serve the salad with cauliflower fried rice.

Variation Tip: Add crushed nuts or corns to the salad.

Nutritional Information Per Serving:

Calories 240 | Fat 14g | Sodium 220mg | Carbs 12g | Fiber 0.2g | Sugar 1g | Protein 7g

Cabbage Mango Slaw

Prep Time: 10 minutes.

Cook Time: 0 minutes.

Serves: 6

Ingredients:

- 3 cups cabbage, shredded
- 1 large mango, pitted and cubed
- ½ cup cilantro, chopped
- ¼ cup red onion, diced
- 1 jalapeño, chopped
- 2 teaspoons olive oil
- 1 orange, zest and juice
- 1 lime juice
- ½ teaspoon salt

Preparation:

1. Mix shredded cabbage with mango and the rest of the ingredients in a salad bowl.
2. Serve.

Serving Suggestion: Serve the salad with grilled tofu steaks.

Variation Tip: Add crushed nuts to the salad.

Nutritional Information Per Serving:

Calories 280 | Fat 8g | Sodium 339mg | Carbs 26g | Fiber 1g | Sugar 2g | Protein 2g

Quinoa Crunch Salad

Prep Time: 10 minutes.

Cook Time: 0 minutes.

Serves: 6

Ingredients:

- 4 cups cooked quinoa
- 1 cup pomegranate seeds
- 4 scallions, chopped
- 1 cup Italian parsley, chopped
- ½ cup toasted almonds, sliced
- ½ orange, zest and juice
- ⅓ cup olive oil
- ½ teaspoon salt
- ¼ teaspoon cracked black pepper
- ¼ teaspoon cinnamon
- ¼ teaspoon allspice
- 2 apples, sliced

Preparation:

1. Mix quinoa with scallions, almond and the rest of the ingredients in a salad bowl.
2. Serve fresh.

Serving Suggestion: Serve the salad with tomato soup

Variation Tip: Add chopped berries to the salad.

Nutritional Information Per Serving:

Calories 261 | Fat 16g |Sodium 189mg | Carbs 23g | Fiber 0.3g | Sugar 18.2g | Protein 3.3g

Fennel Salad with Cucumber

Prep Time: 15 minutes.

Cook Time: 0 minutes.

Serves: 6

Ingredients:

- 2 fennel bulbs, cored and sliced
- 3 Persian cucumbers
- ½ cup fresh dill, chopped
- ¼ cup white onion, sliced
- ⅓ cup olive oil
- 3 tablespoons lemon juice
- Salt to taste
- Black pepper to taste

Preparation:

1. Mix fennel with the rest of the ingredients in a salad bowl.
2. Cover and refrigerate this salad for 15 minutes.
3. Serve

Serving Suggestion: Serve the salad with white bean soup

Variation Tip: Add crushed nuts or chopped cranberries to the salad.

Nutritional Information Per Serving:

Calories 205 | Fat 20g |Sodium 941mg | Carbs 6.1g | Fiber 0.9g | Sugar 0.9g | Protein 5.2g

Curry Tofu Salad

Prep Time: 15 minutes.
Cook Time: 10 minutes.
Serves: 6

Ingredients:

- 8 ounces tofu, cubed
- 1 tablespoon olive oil
- ¼ teaspoon salt
- 1 pinch black pepper
- ¼ cup cashews, chopped
- ¼ cup golden raisins
- ½ cup celery, chopped
- ¼ cup red onion, diced
- ½ cup apple, diced
- ¼ cup cilantro, chopped
- ½ teaspoon cayenne pepper
- 3 teaspoons curry powder
- 3 tablespoons vegan mayo
- 1 tablespoon honey
- 1 tablespoon apple cider vinegar
- Salt and black pepper to taste

Preparation:

1. Pat dry the tofu block and dice it into cubes.
2. Sauté these tofu cubes with oil, black pepper and salt in a skillet until golden brown.
3. Mix cilantro, cashews, celery, apple, onions and raisins in a salad bowl.
4. Whisk vinegar, honey, mayo and spices in a bowl and add to the salad.
5. Mix well and toss in golden brown tofu.
6. Serve

Serving Suggestion: Serve the salad with broccoli spinach soup

Variation Tip: Add crushed nuts to the salad.

Nutritional Information Per Serving:

Calories 245 | Fat 7.9g |Sodium 581mg | Carbs 4g | Fiber 2.6g | Sugar 0.1g | Protein 2.5g

Farro Tabbouleh Salad

Prep Time: 15 minutes.

Cook Time: 10 minutes.

Serves: 6

Ingredients:

- 4 cups cooked Farro
- 1 bunch Italian parsley, chopped
- ¼ cup mint, chopped
- 1 English cucumber, diced
- 1-pound cherry tomatoes, cut in half
- ⅓ cup red onion, diced
- ¼ cup olive oil
- ⅛ cup lemon juice
- ¾ teaspoon kosher salt

Preparation:

1. Mix Farro and the rest of the ingredients in a salad bowl.
2. Serve fresh.

Serving Suggestion: Serve the salad with tomato soup.

Variation Tip: Add crushed nuts or chopped cranberries to the salad.

Nutritional Information Per Serving:

Calories 219 | Fat 13g |Sodium 432mg | Carbs 9.1g | Fiber 3g | Sugar 1g | Protein 3g

Kohlrabi Slaw with Cilantro

Prep Time: 10 minutes.

Cook Time: 0 minutes.

Serves: 6

Ingredients:

- 6 cups kohlrabi, cut into matchsticks
- ½ cup cilantro, chopped
- ½ jalapeño, minced
- ¼ cup scallion, chopped
- Zest from 1 orange
- Juice from 1 orange
- Zest and juice from 1 lime
- Citrus Dressing:
- ¼ cup olive oil
- ¼ cup orange juice
- ⅛ cup lime juice
- ¼ cup honey
- ½ teaspoon kosher salt
- 1 tablespoon rice wine vinegar

Preparation:

1. Mix all the citrus dressing ingredients in a salad bowl.
2. Toss in kohlrabi and the rest of the ingredients, then mix well.
3. Serve.

Serving Suggestion: Serve the salad with cauliflower soup

Variation Tip: Add crushed nuts or chopped berries to the salad

Nutritional Information Per Serving:

Calories 334 | Fat 16g |Sodium 462mg | Carbs 3g | Fiber 0.4g | Sugar 3g | Protein 3.3g

Thai Noodle Salad

Prep Time: 15 minutes.

Cook Time: 10 minutes.

Serves: 6

Ingredients:

- 6 ounces dry rice noodles
- 4 cups mix of carrots, cabbage and radish, shredded
- 1 red bell pepper, sliced
- 3 scallions, sliced
- ½ bunch cilantro, chopped
- 1 tablespoon jalapeño, chopped
- ½ cup crushed peanuts, roasted
- Thai Peanut Sauce
- 3 ginger slices
- 1 garlic clove, chopped
- ¼ cup peanut butter
- ¼ cup fresh orange juice
- 3 tablespoons fresh lime juice
- 2 tablespoons soy sauce
- 3 tablespoons honey
- 3 tablespoons toasted sesame oil
- 1 teaspoon cayenne pepper

Preparation:

1. Boil pasta as per the package's instructions, then drain.
2. For the peanut sauce, blend all the ingredients in a blender until smooth.
3. Toss pasta with all the veggies and peanut sauce in a salad bowl.
4. Serve.

Serving Suggestion: Serve the salad with tomato soup

Variation Tip: Add crushed nuts or chopped cranberries to the salad.

Nutritional Information Per Serving:

Calories 305 | Fat 25g | Sodium 532mg | Carbs 23g | Fiber 0.4g | Sugar 2g | Protein 8.3g

Chapter 5: Dips and Sauces Recipes

Spinach Dip

Prep Time: **15 minutes.**
Cook Time: **6 minutes.**
Serves: **8**

Ingredients:

- 2 teaspoons oil
- 1 small onion, chopped
- 5 garlic cloves, minced
- 6 ounces fresh baby spinach, chopped
- 1½ cup coconut cream
- ½ cup vegan mayo
- ¼ teaspoon paprika
- Salt to taste
- Black pepper to taste

Preparation:

1. In a suitable pan, heat the oil on medium heat.
2. Add in the chopped onion and sauté until translucent.
3. Stir in the garlic and sauté for another minute.
4. Stir in spinach then sauté for 1 minute.
5. Transfer to a bowl and add rest of the ingredients.
6. Mix well and serve.

Serving Suggestion: Serve the dip with crispy fries.

Variation Tip: Add crushed red pepper and a drizzle of olive oil on top before serving.

Nutritional Information Per Serving:

Calories 115 | Fat 16g |Sodium 431mg | Carbs 12g | Fiber 1.2g | Sugar 4g | Protein 3g

Ranch Dressing

Prep Time: 10 minutes.

Cook Time: 0 minutes.

Serves: 8

Ingredients:

- 1½ cup vegan mayo
- ½ cup almond milk
- 1½ teaspoon apple cider vinegar
- 3 garlic cloves, crushed
- ½ tablespoon dried parsley
- 1 teaspoon dried dill
- 1 teaspoon onion powder
- ¼ teaspoon paprika
- ¼ teaspoon black pepper
- Salt, to taste

Preparation:

1. Add mayo, milk and the rest of the ingredients to a small bowl.
2. Mix all the ingredients together until smooth.
3. Serve.

Serving Suggestion: Serve the dressing over a bowl of kale salad.

Variation Tip: Add crushed red pepper on top before serving.

Nutritional Information Per Serving:

Calories 125 | Fat 14g | Sodium 411mg | Carbs 4g | Fiber 0.3g | Sugar 1g | Protein 8.3g

Buffalo Dip

Prep Time: 10 minutes.

Cook Time: 0 minutes.

Serves: 8

Ingredients:

- 1 cup cauliflower, shredded
- 1 (8-ounce) coconut cream
- ½ cup vegan ranch
- ½ cup cayenne pepper hot sauce
- ½ cup vegan cheese, shredded

Preparation:

1. Add coconut cream and ranch, hot sauce and cheese to a blender.
2. Puree the ingredients together until smooth.
3. Stir in shredded cauliflower and mix with a spoon
4. Serve.

Serving Suggestion: Serve the dip with crispy nachos.

Variation Tip: Add crushed red pepper on top before serving.

Nutritional Information Per Serving:

Calories 225 | Fat 15g |Sodium 345mg | Carbs 2.3g | Fiber 1.4g | Sugar 3g | Protein 3.3g

Broccoli Dip

Prep Time: 15 minutes.
Cook Time: 25 minutes.
Serves: **8**

Ingredients:

- 1 cup white beans, drained
- 1 cup cashews, soaked
- 1 tablespoon lemon juice
- 1 tablespoon tapioca starch
- 2 tablespoons nutritional yeast
- 1 teaspoon garlic powder
- 1 teaspoon onion powder
- ½ teaspoon paprika
- Salt, to taste
- 1 pinch red pepper flakes
- 1¼ cup almond milk
- 1½ cups fresh broccoli, florets

Preparation:

1. At 375 degrees F, preheat your oven.
2. Spread broccoli in a baking sheet.
3. Blend rest of the dip ingredients in a blender until smooth.
4. Spread this mixture over the broccoli and bake for 25 minutes.
5. Serve.

Serving Suggestion: Serve the dip with crispy nachos.

Variation Tip: Add roasted broccoli on top before serving.

Nutritional Information Per Serving:

Calories 391 | Fat 5g |Sodium 88mg | Carbs 13g | Fiber 0g | Sugar 0g | Protein 7g

Roasted Cauliflower Dip

Prep Time: 15 minutes.
Cook Time: 20 minutes.
Serves: 8

Ingredients:

- 4 cups cauliflower florets
- 2 jalapeños, sliced
- 2 teaspoons curry powder
- 2 tablespoons olive oil

Blending:

- ⅓ cup olive oil
- 1 tablespoon lemon juice
- 2 garlic cloves
- ½ teaspoon dried cilantro
- ½ teaspoon salt
- ¼ teaspoon black pepper

Preparation:

1. Toss cauliflower with jalapeños and 2 tablespoons olive oil on a baking sheet.
2. Drizzle curry powder on top and bake for 20 minutes in the oven at 400 °F.
3. Puree the cauliflower mixture with the rest of the ingredients in a blender.
4. Serve.

Serving Suggestion: Serve the dip with crispy fries.

Variation Tip: Add crushed red pepper on top before serving.

Nutritional Information Per Serving:

Calories 376 | Fat 21g |Sodium 476mg | Carbs 22g | Fiber 3g | Sugar 4g | Protein 0g

Eggplant Dip

Prep Time: 15 minutes.
Cook Time: 10 minutes.
Serves: 8

Ingredients:

- 2 eggplants, sliced
- 3 tablespoons olive oil
- 3 tablespoons roasted tahini
- 2 garlic cloves, chopped
- ½ teaspoon ground cumin
- Juice of 1 lemon
- Salt and cayenne pepper to taste
- 1 tablespoon parsley, chopped

Preparation:

1. Slice and rub the eggplant with olive oil.
2. Grill these eggplant slices for 5 minutes per side.
3. Peel and puree the eggplant slices in the blender.
4. Add rest of the ingredients then blend again.
5. Serve.

Serving Suggestion: Serve the dip with crispy nachos.

Variation Tip: Add crushed red pepper on top before serving.

Nutritional Information Per Serving:

Calories 380 | Fat 20g |Sodium 686mg | Carbs 13g | Fiber 1g | Sugar 1.2g | Protein 2g

Chapter 6: Lunch Recipes

Coconut Green Soup

Prep Time: 15 minutes.
Cook Time: 17 minutes.
Serves: 4

Ingredients:

- 1 teaspoon whole cumin seeds
- 1 teaspoon whole coriander seeds
- 2 teaspoons coconut oil
- 1 large shallot, chopped
- 1 medium zucchini, chopped
- 1 small bunch celery, chopped
- 1 medium apple, peeled, cored and chopped
- 3-inch ginger, peeled and chopped
- 6 cups vegetable stock
- Salt and black pepper, to taste
- 4 cups greens, chopped
- 1 (14-ounce) can full fat coconut milk
- 2 tablespoons lime juice
- Garnishing
- Cooked brown rice
- Cooked lentils or chickpeas
- Sliced ripe avocado
- Coconut milk
- Chilli-infused olive oil
- Chopped basil

Preparation:

1. Roast coriander seeds and cumin in a skillet for 1 minute then transfer to a grinder and grind.
2. Sauté shallots with coconut oil in a saucepan for 3 minutes.
3. Stir in apple, celery, zucchini, ginger, coriander powder and cumin powder.
4. Sauté for 3 minutes, then add vegetable stock, black pepper and salt.
5. Boil, reduce its heat and cook for 10 minutes.
6. Stir in coconut milk, and chopped greens, then cook for 3 minutes.
7. Puree this soup with a hand blender until smooth.
8. Add lime juice and mix well.

9. Serve warm with favorite garnishes on top.

Serving Suggestion: Serve the soup with boiled cauliflower rice or grilled zucchini.

Variation Tip: Add crushed or sliced almonds on top before serving.

Nutritional Information Per Serving:
Calories 361 | Fat 16g |Sodium 515mg | Carbs 18g | Fiber 0.1g | Sugar 18.2g | Protein 33.3g

Roasted Cauliflower Soup

Prep Time: 15 minutes.
Cook Time: 1 hr. 15 minutes.
Serves: 4

Ingredients:

- 1 cauliflower head, cut into florets
- 1 lb. Yukon gold potatoes, scrubbed
- 2 yellow onions, skin removed
- 2 tablespoons rosemary leaves
- 2 tablespoons olive oil
- Salt and black pepper, to taste
- 1 tablespoon fresh lemon juice
- 6 cups vegetable stock
- Olive oil
- Croutons
- Nuts, toasted and chopped
- Leafy herbs, chopped
- Balsamic reduction
- Squeezes of lemon
- Black pepper

Preparation:

1. Preheat your oven to 400°F.
2. Spread the cauliflower florets, onion and potatoes in a baking sheet.
3. Sprinkle oil, black pepper, salt and rosemary on top, then toss well.
4. Roast these veggies for 1 hour and toss them after every 10 minutes.
5. Puree veggies with lemon juice and vegetable stock in a blender.
6. Transfer this blend to a saucepan and cook to a boil.
7. Add more stock or water if needed.
8. Serve warm.

Serving Suggestion: Serve the soup with cucumber salad on the side.

Variation Tip: Add toasted nuts and seeds on top before serving.

Nutritional Information Per Serving:

Calories 405 | Fat 22.7g | Sodium 227mg | Carbs 36g | Fiber 1.4g | Sugar 0.9g | Protein 45.2g

Squash and Chestnut Soup

Prep Time: 15 minutes.
Cook Time: 55 minutes.
Serves: 4

Ingredients:

- 1 lb. chestnuts
- 2 tablespoons olive oil
- 1 onion, chopped
- 4 garlic cloves, chopped
- 1 teaspoon salt
- 7 cups water
- 1 large sage sprig
- 3 bay leaves
- 2 teaspoons tamari soy sauce
- 1 kabocha squash, peeled, seeded and diced
- Black pepper, to taste
- Kale Sesame Crisps
- 1 bunch Lacinato kale, leaves separated
- 2 teaspoons olive oil
- 1 teaspoon maple syrup
- Salt and black pepper, to taste
- 2 tablespoons sesame seeds

Preparation:

1. Preheat your oven to 425°F.
2. Make a slit on top of each chestnut and add them to a saucepan.
3. Pour enough water to cover them, and cook to a boil then drain.
4. Spread these chestnuts in a baking sheet and roast for 20 minutes.
5. Allow them to cool then peel off their shells.
6. Reduce the oven's heat to 400 °F.
7. Toss kale leaves with black pepper, salt, 2 teaspoons olive oil and maple syrup in a baking sheet.
8. Drizzle sesame seeds on top and bake for 8 minutes.
9. Sauté onion with olive oil in a soup pan over medium heat for 6 minutes.
10. Add garlic and sauté for 30 seconds.
11. Stir in bay leaves, sage, water, chestnuts, squash, and salt then cook to a boil.
12. Reduce its heat and cook for 20 minutes.
13. Puree this soup with a blender in batches then return to the pot.
14. Stir in black pepper, salt and tamari and boil again.
15. Garnish with kale chips.
16. Serve warm.

Serving Suggestion: Serve the soup with toasted bread croutons.

Variation Tip: You can replace kale chips with zucchini chips.

Nutritional Information Per Serving:

Calories 345 | Fat 36g | Sodium 272mg | Carbs 41g | Fiber 0.2g | Sugar 0.1g | Protein 22.5g

Shiitake Tortilla Soup

Prep Time: 15 minutes.
Cook Time: 30 minutes.
Serves: 4

Ingredients:

- 6 (6-inch) corn tortillas
- 2 tablespoons avocado oil
- 1 (15-ounce) can crushed tomatoes
- 4 cups vegetable stock
- 1 small white onion, diced
- 4 garlic cloves, minced
- 1 jalapeño, minced
- ½ teaspoon dried Mexican oregano
- 1 teaspoon cumin
- 1 teaspoon chipotle powder
- ¾ lb. shiitake mushrooms, sliced
- 1 (15-ounce) can black beans, drained
- 1 cup corn kernels
- Salt and black pepper, to taste
- Serve
- Ripe avocado, diced
- Cilantro, chopped
- Lime wedges

Preparation:

1. Cut each tortilla into thin strips and spread them in a greased baking sheet.
2. Bake these tortillas strips for 12 minutes in the oven at 350 degrees.
3. Toss them once cooked halfway and then allow them to cool when cooked.
4. Blend crushed tomatoes with half of the tortilla strips, and 1 cup stock until smooth.
5. Sauté onion with oil in a cooking pot over medium heat for 3 minutes.
6. Stir in chipotle powder, cumin, oregano, jalapeño, and garlic then cook for 30 seconds.
7. Stir in mushrooms and cook for 2 minutes.
8. Add vegetable stock, corn, black beans, black pepper and salt.
9. Stir in blended tomato mixture then cook to a boil.
10. Now, reduce its heat and cook for 10 minutes.
11. Garnish with remaining tortillas strips, cilantro, lime wedges, and avocado.
12. Serve warm.

Serving Suggestion: Serve the soup with sautéed green beans.

Variation Tip: Drizzle vegan cheese on top before serving.

Nutritional Information Per Serving:

Calories 395 | Fat 9.5g |Sodium 655mg | Carbs 34g | Fiber 0.4g | Sugar 0.4g | Protein 28.3g

Vegan Tomato Soup

Prep Time: 10 minutes.

Cook Time: 1 hour 10 minutes.

Serves: 4

Ingredients:

- 4 lbs. tomatoes
- 3 shallots, peeled
- 5 garlic cloves, peeled
- 2 teaspoons fresh thyme leaves
- 2 tablespoons olive oil
- Salt and black pepper, to taste
- ½ cup raw cashews, soaked and drained
- 1 tablespoon tomato paste
- ½ cup basil leaves, packed
- 3 cups vegetable stock
- 1 tablespoon balsamic vinegar

Preparation:

1. Preheat your oven to 350°F. Layer a baking sheet with parchment paper.
2. Spread the tomato pieces in the baking and add garlic cloves on top.
3. Add shallots around the tomato pieces.
4. Drizzle olive oil, black pepper and salt over the veggies.
5. Roast these veggies for 1 hour, then allow them to cool.
6. Blend the roasted tomatoes with cashews, tomato paste, basil, and vegetable stock in a blender until smooth.
7. Transfer this soup to a cooking pan and cook to a boil.
8. Stir in vinegar and garnish with basil and olive oil.
9. Serve warm.

Serving Suggestion: Serve the soup with fresh greens salad.

Variation Tip: Add a drizzle of herbs on top.

Nutritional Information Per Serving:

Calories 301 | Fat 5g | Sodium 340mg | Carbs 37g | Fiber 1.2g | Sugar 1.3g | Protein 15.3g

Pita Pizzas

Prep Time: 15 minutes.
Cook Time: 30 minutes.
Serves: 6

Ingredients:

- 1 cup onion, chopped
- 1 cup bell pepper, chopped
- 2 garlic cloves, minced
- ½ teaspoon ground cumin
- 1 (15-ounce) can black beans, rinsed
- 1 cup fresh corn kernels
- 6 (6-inch) whole-wheat pita rounds
- 1 cup avocado, pitted, peeled and chopped
- 1 cup oil-free salsa
- 2 tablespoons fresh cilantro, snipped

Preparation:

1. Preheat your oven to 350°F.
2. Layer 2 baking sheets with parchment paper.
3. Boil ¼ cup water in a saucepan then stir in cumin, garlic, sweet pepper and onion.
4. Cook on medium-low heat for 10 minutes then add corn and beans then cook for 5 minutes.
5. Mix and mash this mixture a little.
6. Place the pita round in the baking sheets and bake them for 15 minutes.
7. Spread the bean and avocado mixture on top of the pita bread.
8. Garnish with cilantro and salsa.
9. Serve.

Serving Suggestion: Serve the pizzas with kale cucumber salad.

Variation Tip: Add sliced mushrooms and olives over the pizza.

Nutritional Information Per Serving:

Calories 248 | Fat 23g | Sodium 350mg | Carbs 38g | Fiber 6.3g | Sugar 1g | Protein 40.3g

Black Bean Burgers

Prep Time: 15 minutes.
Cook Time: 15 minutes.
Serves: 4

Ingredients:

- 1 cup cooked brown rice
- 1 (15-ounce) can black beans
- ½ onion, diced
- ¼ cup corn
- 1 teaspoon cumin
- 1 teaspoon garlic powder
- ¼ teaspoon chili powder
- ¼ cup cornmeal
- 2 tablespoons salsa

Preparation:

1. Boil rice in 1 cup of water in a saucepan and cook until the rice is soft.
2. Drain and keep the beans aside.
3. In the same pan, boil beans with water until soft then drain.
4. Mash the beans in a bowl and keep them aside.
5. Preheat your oven to 350°F.
6. Layer a baking sheet with wax paper.
7. Sauté onion in a skillet until soft then stir in spices and corn.
8. Toss in veggies, salsa, rice and cornmeal then mix well.
9. Make 4-6 patties out of this mixture and place on a baking sheet lined with parchment paper.
10. Bake the patties for 15 minutes in the preheated oven.
11. Serve warm.

Serving Suggestion: Serve the burgers in toasted burgers buns.

Variation Tip: Use sliced cucumbers, coleslaw and vegan mayo over the patties.

Nutritional Information Per Serving:

Calories 309 | Fat 25g | Sodium 463mg | Carbs 29g | Fiber 0.3g | Sugar 0.3g | Protein 18g

Spinach-Potato Tacos

Prep Time: 15 minutes.

Cook Time: 26 minutes.

Serves: 12

Ingredients:

- 2 Yukon gold potatoes, diced
- 1 (10-ounce) package spinach
- 1 large onion, diced
- 1 medium poblano pepper, seeded and diced
- 2 garlic cloves, minced
- 2 teaspoons ground cumin
- 1 cup almond milk
- 3 tablespoons nutritional yeast
- Salt and black pepper, to taste
- 12 corn tortillas
- ½ cup fresh cilantro, chopped

Preparation:

1. Add potatoes and water to a saucepan and cook for 12 minutes until soft.
2. Drain and keep the potatoes aside.
3. Sauté onion with poblano pepper and 2 tablespoons water in a skillet for 7 minutes.
4. Stir in cumin and garlic then cook for 1 minute.
5. Add potatoes, spinach, yeast, black pepper and salt then cook for 3 minutes.
6. Then remove the cooked mixture from the heat and mix well.
7. Sear the corn tortillas in a skillet for 3-5 minutes per side.
8. Divide the potato mixture on top of the corn tortillas.
9. Roll the tortillas and garnish with cilantro.
10. Serve.

Serving Suggestion: Serve the tacos with mashed cauliflower.

Variation Tip: Add more herbs of your choice to the filling.

Nutritional Information Per Serving:

Calories 337 | Fat 20g | Sodium 719mg | Carbs 51g | Fiber 0.9g | Sugar 1.4g | Protein 37.8g

Sweet Potato Quesadillas

Prep Time: 15 minutes.

Cook Time: 56 minutes.

Serves: 8

Ingredients:

- 1 large sweet potato
- 1 cup brown rice, cooked
- 8 ounces re-fried beans
- 1 cup of salsa
- 1 cup fresh spinach
- 8 ounces black beans, drained and rinsed
- ¼ teaspoon onion powder
- ¼ teaspoon chili powder
- ¼ teaspoon cumin
- 1 jalapeño pepper, diced
- 8 whole-wheat tortillas

Preparation:

1. Preheat your oven to 375 °F.
2. Layer a sheet pan with parchment paper.
3. Peel and dice all the sweet potatoes into quarters.
4. Spread the sweet potato wedges on a baking sheet and bake for 45 minutes.
5. Add rice to a rice cooker and cook as per the package's instructions.
6. Mix the sweet potatoes with spinach, rice and salsa in a saucepan.
7. Stir in refried beans, black beans, chili powder, cumin and onion powder.
8. Divide the sweet potatoes on top of tortillas and roll them.
9. Sear the tortillas roll in the skillet for 3 minutes per side.
10. Cut in half and garnish with salsa.
11. Serve.

Serving Suggestion: Serve the meal with chickpea salad.

Variation Tip: Add paprika for more spice.

Nutritional Information Per Serving:

Calories 448 | Fat 13g | Sodium 353mg | Carbs 33g | Fiber 0.4g | Sugar 1g | Protein 29g

Slow-Cooker Chili

Prep Time: 10 minutes.
Cook Time: 5 hours 15 minutes.
Serves: 6

Ingredients:

- 2 cups pinto beans, rinsed
- 1 (14½-ounce) can fire-roasted diced tomatoes, undrained
- 1 cup red onion, chopped
- 1 (1-ounce) vegetarian chili seasoning
- 6 garlic cloves, minced
- 4 cups vegetable stock
- 2 cups water
- 1 cup fresh whole kernel corn
- Toppings
- Chopped bell pepper
- Sliced green onions
- Snipped fresh cilantro

Preparation:

1. Add beans and all other ingredients, except corn to a slow cooker.
2. Cover and cook this bean Chilli for 5 hours on high heat.
3. Stir in corn then cook for 15 minutes and mix well.
4. Garnish with bell pepper, cilantro, and green onions.
5. Serve warm.

Serving Suggestion: Serve the chili with crushed tortillas chips on top.

Variation Tip: Add minced jalapeños.

Nutritional Information Per Serving:

Calories 376 | Fat 17g | Sodium 1127mg | Carbs 34g | Fiber 1g | Sugar 3g | Protein 29g

Sweet Potato Chili with Kale

Prep Time: 15 minutes.

Cook Time: 43 minutes.

Serves: 6

Ingredients:

- 2 medium sweet potatoes, diced
- 1 large red onion, chopped
- 2 (15-ounce) cans kidney beans
- 2 red bell peppers, seeded and diced
- 2 pounds fresh tomatoes, diced
- 1 tablespoon chili powder
- 2 teaspoons smoked paprika
- ¼ teaspoon chipotle powder
- 2 cups Lacinato kale, shredded
- 3 cups of orange, juiced

Preparation:

1. Sauté onion with bell pepper and orange juice in a skillet for 10 minutes.
2. Stir in the rest of the ingredients, reserving the kale and cook for 30 minutes on medium heat.
3. Mash the cooked mixture a little then add kale.
4. Cook for 3 minutes then serve warm.

Serving Suggestion: Serve the chili with boiled rice.

Variation Tip: Add lemon juice and lemon zest on top.

Nutritional Information Per Serving:

Calories 457 | Fat 19g |Sodium 557mg | Carbs 29g | Fiber 1.8g | Sugar 1.2g | Protein 32.5g

Potato-Cauliflower Curry

Prep Time: 15 minutes.
Cook Time: 39 minutes.
Serves: 4

Ingredients:

- 4 cups cauliflower florets
- 2 cups potato pieces, cubed
- 1 cup onion wedges
- ¼ cup tomato paste
- 1 tablespoon mild curry powder
- 1½ teaspoon fresh ginger, grated
- 1 teaspoon cumin seeds
- 1 garlic clove, minced
- 1½ cups fresh peas
- ¼ cup raw cashews, ground
- 2 tablespoons lime juice
- Cayenne pepper, to taste
- Sea salt, to taste
- 4 cups cooked brown rice
- 1 tablespoon fresh cilantro, snipped

Preparation:

1. Add cauliflower to a steamer basket, cover and cook for 5 minutes.
2. Transfer the cauliflower to a bowl.
3. Add potato pieces to the steamer and cook for 10 minutes.
4. Transfer these potatoes to the cauliflower then mix well.
5. Blend onion wedges with garlic, cumin seeds, ginger, curry powder, and tomato paste in a blender.
6. Pour this mixture into a skillet along with 1 cup water and cook for 7 minutes.
7. Reduce its heat to medium-low heat and cook for 10 minutes until the sauce thickens.
8. Add potatoes, cauliflower and the rest of the ingredients.
9. Mix well and cook for 7 minutes.
10. Garnish with cilantro and serve warm.

Serving Suggestion: Serve the curry with boiled rice.

Variation Tip: Replace potatoes with sweet potatoes.

Nutritional Information Per Serving:

Calories 392 | Fat 16g | Sodium 466mg | Carbs 39g | Fiber 0.9g | Sugar 0.6g | Protein 48g

Zucchini and Chickpea Sauté

Prep Time: 15 minutes.

Cook Time: 25 minutes.

Serves: 6

Ingredients:

- 1 onion, chopped
- 1 large red bell pepper, chopped
- 6 garlic cloves, minced
- 1 teaspoon dried oregano
- ½ teaspoon dried thyme
- 1 cup oil-free marinara sauce
- 1 tablespoon white wine vinegar
- Salt and black pepper, to taste
- 3 medium zucchinis, halved lengthwise and sliced
- 1 15-ounce can chickpeas, rinsed and drained
- 10 fresh basil leaves, chopped

Preparation:

1. Sauté onion, bell pepper, garlic, oregano, and thyme in a greased skillet for 10 minutes.
2. Stir in zucchini and cook for 10 minutes.
3. Stir in vinegar, marinara sauce, black pepper, salt and chickpeas.
4. Cook the mixture for 5 minutes then garnish with basil.
5. Serve warm.

Serving Suggestion: Serve the chickpeas sauté with fried cauliflower rice.

Variation Tip: Add some diced tofu to the sauté.

Nutritional Information Per Serving:

Calories 321 | Fat 7.4g |Sodium 356mg | Carbs 23g | Fiber 2.4g | Sugar 5g | Protein 37.2g

Raw Collard Wraps

Prep Time: 15 minutes.

Cook Time: 0 minutes.

Serves: 3

Ingredients:

- 4 large collard leaves
- 1 red bell pepper, julienned
- 1 avocado
- 3 ounces alfalfa sprouts
- ½ lime, juiced
- 1 cup raw pecans, chopped
- 1 tablespoon tamari
- ½ teaspoon garlic, minced
- ½ teaspoon ginger, grated
- 1 teaspoon olive oil

Preparation:

1. Soak the leaves in warm water for 10 minutes then drain.
2. Puree cumin with olive oil, tamari and pecans in a blender.
3. Spread the collard leaf on the working surface and top them with the pecan's mixture.
4. Divide the avocado slices, red pepper slices and alfalfa sprouts on top.
5. Drizzle the lime juice on top and roll the leaves.
6. Cut the roll in half and serve.

Serving Suggestion: Serve the wraps with vegan spinach dip.

Variation Tip: Add grilled tofu to the wraps.

Nutritional Information Per Serving:

Calories 332 | Fat 10g |Sodium 994mg | Carbs 21g | Fiber 0.4g | Sugar 3g | Protein 8g

Avocado Chickpea Lettuce Cups

Prep Time: 10 minutes.

Cook Time: 0 minutes.

Serves: 6

Ingredients:

- 1 tablespoon Dijon mustard
- 1 tablespoon shallots, minced
- 1 lime, juiced
- 2 tablespoons fresh cilantro, chopped
- 1 tablespoon apple cider vinegar
- 2½ tablespoons olive oil
- 1 can chickpeas, drained
- 8 ounces jarred hearts of palm, drained
- ½ cup fresh cucumber, diced
- 2 small avocados, peeled, seeded and diced
- 4 handfuls of mixed greens
- Salt and black pepper to taste

Preparation:

1. Mix shallots with apple cider vinegar, cilantro, lime zest and juice in a bowl.
2. Stir in oil, black pepper and salt then mix well.
3. Add cucumber, heart of palm and chickpeas then mix well.
4. Fold in avocados and greens then mix again.
5. Serve.

Serving Suggestion: Serve the lettuce cups with mashed cauliflower.

Variation Tip: Add crumbled tofu to the filling.

Nutritional Information Per Serving:

Calories 285 | Fat 8g |Sodium 146mg | Carbs 35g | Fiber 0.1g | Sugar 0.4g | Protein 1g

Chapter 7: Dinner Recipes

Lime Bean Artichoke Wraps

Prep Time: 10 minutes.
Cook Time: 10 minutes.
Serves: 2

Ingredients:

- Lima bean spread
- 1 cup cooked baby lima beans
- 2 tablespoons nutritional yeast
- 2 tablespoons parsley, chopped
- ½ teaspoon garlic, minced
- ½ teaspoon onion powder
- 2 teaspoons fresh lime juice
- 2 teaspoons white balsamic vinegar
- Wraps
- 2 gluten-free vegan wraps
- 1 cup raw broccoli, sliced lengthwise
- 2 whole hearts of palm, sliced lengthwise

Preparation:

1. Blend lime beans with yeast, parsley, garlic, onion powder, lime juice and vinegar in a blender until smooth.
2. Spread the beans mixture on top of the wraps and top them with broccoli and hearts of palm.
3. Roll the wraps like a burrito and cut in half.
4. Grill the wraps in the grill over high heat for 5 minutes per side.
5. Serve.

Serving Suggestion: Serve the wraps with roasted veggies on the side.

Variation Tip: Add chopped spinach to filling.

Nutritional Information Per Serving:
Calories 324 | Fat 1g |Sodium 236mg | Carbs 42g | Fiber 0.3g | Sugar 0.1g | Protein 1g

Butternut Squash Lasagna

Prep Time: 10 minutes.

Cook Time: 1 hour 40 minutes.

Serves: 6

Ingredients:

- 2 tablespoons olive oil
- 2 pounds butternut squash, cubed
- ½ cup water
- 4 amaretti cookies, crumbled
- 8 ounces shiitake mushrooms, sliced
- ¼ cup butter
- ¼ cup whole-wheat flour
- 3½ cups almond milk
- ½ teaspoon ground nutmeg
- 1 cup fresh basil leaves
- 13 ounces DeLillo no-boil lasagna noodles
- 3 cups vegan cheese, shredded
- Salt and black pepper, to taste

Preparation:

1. Preheat your oven to 375°F .
2. Sauté squash with black pepper, salt and oil in a skillet for 5 minutes.
3. Add water to the squash, cover and cook for about 20 minutes on medium heat.
4. Blend the squash with amaretti in a blender until smooth.
5. Sauté mushrooms with oil and ¼ teaspoons salt in a skillet for 10 minutes.
6. Mix butter with flour in a skillet for 1 minute.
7. Pour in milk, mix well until lump-free then boil the mixture.
8. Stir in black pepper, nutmeg and ¼ teaspoons salt.
9. Mix well then cook for about 5 minutes until the sauce thickens.
10. Add basil and blend well with a blender.
11. Grease a 13x9 -inch baking dish with butter.
12. Spread ¾ cup sauce in the baking dish.
13. Arrange the lasagna noodles at the bottom of this dish.
14. Top the noodles with ⅓ squash puree and add ⅓ mushroom on top.
15. Drizzle 1 cup vegan cheese on top.
16. Repeat all the layers and cover this dish with foil sheet.
17. Bake the prepared lasagna for 40 minutes in the oven.
18. Remove the tin foil from the top and bake for another 15 minutes.
19. Serve warm.

Serving Suggestion: Serve the lasagna with mashed cauliflower.

Variation Tip: You can replace lasagna noodles with zucchini slices

Nutritional Information Per Serving:

Calories 438 | Fat 7g |Sodium 316mg | Carbs 34g | Fiber 0.3g | Sugar 0.3g | Protein 3g

Sweet Potato Penne Pasta

Prep Time: 15 minutes.

Cook Time: 15 minutes.

Serves: 6

Ingredients:

Sauce:

- ½ cup cashews
- 1 roasted sweet potato, peeled
- ⅔ cup water
- 2 garlic cloves
- 1 chipotle pepper
- ⅛ teaspoon nutmeg
- ½ teaspoon sea salt
- Black pepper, to taste

Pasta:

- 3 cups of quinoa penne
- Mushrooms
- ½ tablespoon olive oil
- 1 cup baby bella mushrooms, sliced
- ¼ teaspoon garlic powder
- Salt and black pepper, to taste

Preparation:

1. Soak cashews in 4 cups water in a bowl for 2 hours then drain.
2. Blend cashews with black pepper, salt, nutmeg, chili pepper, garlic, water, and sweet potato in a blender until smooth.
3. Boil pasta in a boiling water in a cooking pot as per the package's instructions.
4. Drain the pasta and transfer to the pot.
5. Sauté mushrooms with oil, black pepper, salt and garlic powder in a skillet for 5 minutes.
6. Add the sweet potato sauce and pasta then mix well.
7. Garnish with sage.
8. Serve warm.

Serving Suggestion: Serve the pasta with roasted broccoli florets.

Variation Tip: Drizzle lemon juice on top before cooking.

Nutritional Information Per Serving:

Calories 456 | Fat 4g | Sodium 634mg | Carbs 31g | Fiber 1.4g | Sugar 1g | Protein 3g

Roasted Butternut Squash Pasta

Prep Time: 15 minutes.
Cook Time: 35 minutes.
Serves: 4

Ingredients:

- ½ tablespoon olive oil
- 4 cups butternut squash, cubed
- 2 garlic cloves, unpeeled
- Salt and black pepper, to taste
- 8 ounces brown rice pasta
- 2 tablespoons vegan cream cheese
- 1 cup almond milk
- ½ cup frozen peas, thawed

Preparation:

1. Preheat your oven to 400°F .
2. Toss butternut squash with oil, black pepper and salt in a baking pan.
3. Add garlic and roast for 30 minutes.
4. Cook the pasta as per the package's instruction then drain.
5. Peel the roasted garlic and add to a blender along with squash, salt, black pepper, almond milk and vegan cream cheese then blend until smooth.
6. Add peas and squash sauce to the pasta and serve.

Serving Suggestion: Serve the pasta with crumbled tofu on top.

Variation Tip: Add garlic salt on top for more taste.

Nutritional Information Per Serving:

Calories 449 | Fat 31g |Sodium 723mg | Carbs 32g | Fiber 2.5g | Sugar 2g | Protein 26g

Cashew Mac and Cheese

Prep Time: 15 minutes.
Cook Time: 10 minutes.
Serves: 4

Ingredients:

- 1½ cups raw cashews
- 2 garlic cloves
- ½ cup nutritional yeast
- 1¼ cups almond milk
- 1 jalapeño, chopped
- ¾ teaspoon ground turmeric
- ¾ teaspoon paprika
- ½ teaspoon onion powder
- 1 teaspoon Dijon mustard
- 1 teaspoon salt
- Black pepper, to taste
- 1-pound shell Conchiglie pasta

Preparation:

1. Soak cashews in 4 cups water in a bowl for 2 hours then drain.
2. Drain and blend the cashews with black pepper, salt, mustard, onion powder, paprika, turmeric, jalapeño, almond milk, yeast, and garlic in a blender until smooth.
3. Cook the noodles as per the package's instructions then drain.
4. Mix the noodles with the cashews sauce in a bowl.
5. Garnish with black pepper.
6. Serve warm.

Serving Suggestion: Serve the mac and cheese with mashed sweet potatoes.

Variation Tip: Add a drizzle of taco seasoning on top.

Nutritional Information Per Serving:

Calories 310 | Fat 6g | Sodium 220mg | Carbs 31g | Fiber 2.4g | Sugar 1.2g | Protein 12g

Taco Pasta with Sweet Corn

Prep Time: 15 minutes.

Cook Time: 10 minutes.

Serves: 6

Ingredients:

Pasta cheese sauce:

- ¾ cup cashews
- ¾ cup water
- 1 garlic clove
- 2 tablespoons lime juice
- 2½ teaspoons cumin
- 2 teaspoons chili powder
- 1 teaspoon dried oregano
- ½ teaspoon paprika
- ⅛ teaspoon cayenne pepper
- ¾ teaspoon salt

Pasta:

- 8 ounces large elbow noodles
- 1 (15-ounce) can black beans, rinsed
- 1¼ cups Birds Eye Sweet Corn, cooked
- ¾ cup chunky salsa

Preparation:

1. Soak cashews in 2 cups of water for 2 hours then drain.
2. Blend cashews with paprika, oregano, chili powder, cumin, lime juice, garlic, and ½ cup of water.
3. Boil the pasta as per the package's instruction then drain.
4. Return the pasta to a cooking pot then add cashew sauce, corn, salsa and beans.
5. Mix well and garnish with all the toppings.
6. Serve warm.

Serving Suggestion: Serve the pasta with mashed cauliflower

Variation Tip: Add hot sauce for tangy taste.

Nutritional Information Per Serving:

Calories 382 | Fat 6g | Sodium 620mg | Carbs 15g | Fiber 2g | Sugar 1.2g | Protein 12g

Vegetarian Lentil Loaf

Prep Time: 15 minutes.

Cook Time: 1 hr. 23 minutes.

Serves: 6

Ingredients:

- 1 cup dry green lentils
- 4 cups water
- 3 tablespoons flaxseed meal
- ⅓ cup water
- ½ tablespoon olive oil
- 4 garlic cloves, minced
- 1 small white or yellow onion, diced
- 1 red bell pepper, diced
- 1 carrot, diced
- 1 jalapeño, seeded and diced
- 2 teaspoons cumin
- 1 teaspoon chili powder
- ½ teaspoon paprika
- ½ teaspoon garlic powder
- ½ teaspoon onion powder
- ¼ teaspoon coriander
- ½ cup gluten free rolled oats
- ½ cup gluten free oat flour
- ½ cup fresh cilantro, chopped
- 1 teaspoon salt
- Black pepper, to taste
- Glaze:
- ½ cup ketchup
- ½ teaspoon yellow mustard
- ½ teaspoon apple cider vinegar
- ¼ teaspoon chipotle chili powder

Preparation:

1. Rinse and add lentils to a cooking pot with 4 cups of water.
2. Add a dash of salt and cook for 30 minutes on a simmer then drain.
3. Mix ⅓ cup water and flaxseed meal in a bowl.
4. Preheat your oven to 350°F.
5. Grease a loaf pan with cooking spray.
6. Sauté garlic, jalapeño, cilantro, carrot, bell pepper, onion with oil in a suitable skillet for 7 minutes.

7. Stir in spices and cook for 30 seconds.
8. Blend the 2 cups of cooked lentils in a blender until smooth.
9. Return the lentils to the cooking pot and add the veggies.
10. Stir in the rest of the ingredients then mix well.
11. Prepare the glaze by mixing its ingredients in a bowl.
12. Brush the glaze over the meatloaf.
13. Spread the mixture in a meatloaf pan and bake for 45 minutes.
14. Allow it to cool then slice.
15. Serve warm.

Serving Suggestion: Serve the lentil loaf with roasted vegetables.

Variation Tip: Add corns to the lentil loaf.

Nutritional Information Per Serving:
Calories 93 | Fat 3g | Sodium 510mg | Carbs 22g | Fiber 3g | Sugar 4g | Protein 4g

Black Bean Loaf with Avocado Sauce

Prep Time: 15 minutes.
Cook Time: 42 minutes.
Serves: 6

Ingredients:

- 3 tablespoons flaxseed meal
- ½ cup water
- 1 teaspoon olive oil
- 1 small yellow onion
- 3 garlic cloves, minced
- 1 red bell pepper, finely diced
- 1 carrot, shredded
- 1 jalapeño, seeded and diced
- 2 teaspoons cumin
- 1 tablespoon chili powder
- 1 teaspoon dried oregano
- ¼ teaspoon cayenne pepper
- ¼ cup cilantro, diced
- 2 (15-ounce) cans black beans, rinsed
- ¾ cup sweet corn organic preferred
- ½ cup gluten free oats

- ½ cup gluten free oat flour
- Salt and black pepper, to taste
- Sauce:
- ⅓ cup salsa Verde green salsa
- ½ avocado, mashed
- 2 tablespoons cilantro, chopped

Preparation:

1. Preheat your oven to 350°F.
2. Layer a 9-inch loaf pan with cooking spray.
3. Mix ½ cup water with flaxseed meal in a bowl then leave for 10 minutes.
4. Sauté garlic, jalapeño, carrots, bell pepper, and onion with 1 teaspoon oil in a skillet for 7 minutes.
5. Blend beans with sautéed veggies, black pepper, salt and rest of the ingredients along with flaxseeds.
6. Spread this meatloaf mixture in the pan and bake for 35 minutes in the oven.
7. Allow the meatloaf to cool then slice.
8. Mix salsa with cilantro and avocado in a bowl.
9. Add this sauce over the meatloaf.
10. Serve warm

Serving Suggestion: Serve the bean loaf with sautéed vegetables on the side.

Variation Tip: Add boiled peas to the bean loaf.

Nutritional Information Per Serving:

Calories 378 | Fat 3.8g | Sodium 620mg | Carbs 33g | Fiber 2.4g | Sugar 1.2g | Protein 5.4g

Pineapple Tofu Kabobs

Prep Time: 10 minutes.

Cook Time: 10 minutes.

Serves: 4

Ingredients:

- 2 tablespoons tamari
- 1 teaspoon apple cider vinegar
- 2 tablespoons fresh pineapple juice
- 2 teaspoons ginger, grated
- 2 garlic cloves, minced
- ½ teaspoon ground turmeric
- 1 (14-ounce) package Nagoya extra firm tofu
- 2 cups fresh pineapple, cubed

Garnish

- Fresh chopped cilantro
- Diced onion
- Hot sauce

Preparation:

1. Pat dry the tofu block with a paper towel and cut into cubes.
2. Mix tamari, turmeric, garlic, ginger, pineapple juice, and apple cider vinegar in a large bowl.
3. Toss in tofu cubes then mix well and cover to marinate for 30 minutes.
4. Set a grill over medium high heat and grease its grilling grates.
5. Thread tofu and pineapple on the skewers and grill the skewers for 5 minutes per side.
6. Garnish with hot sauce, green onion and cilantro.
7. Serve warm.

Serving Suggestion: Serve the tofu kebobs with mashed cauliflower.

Variation Tip: Brush the kebabs with sriracha sauce for seasoning.

Nutritional Information Per Serving's

Calories 304 | Fat 31g |Sodium 834mg | Carbs 27g | Fiber 0.2g | Sugar 0.3g | Protein 4.6g

Lentil Sloppy Joes with Spaghetti Squash

Prep Time: 10 minutes.

Cook Time: 4 hours.

Serves: 4

Ingredients:

- 1¼ cups uncooked green lentils, rinsed
- 1 white onion, diced
- 1 red pepper, diced
- 1 carrot, sliced
- 3 garlic cloves, minced
- 1½ tablespoons chili powder
- 1 teaspoon cumin
- ½ teaspoon onion powder
- ¼ teaspoon cayenne pepper
- 1 (15-ounce) can tomato sauce
- 1 (15-ounce) can diced tomatoes
- 1½ cups water
- 2 tablespoons organic ketchup
- 1 teaspoon yellow mustard
- 1 spaghetti squash, halved and seeded
- 1 teaspoon soy sauce
- Salt and black pepper, to taste

Preparation:

1. Add all the ingredients except spaghetti squash to a slow cooker.
2. Mix well and place the spaghetti squash on top.
3. Cover and slow-cook on high for 4 hours on High heat.
4. Remove the squash from the top and shred the flesh.
5. Transfer the flesh to a serving plate and then top it with lentils mixture.
6. Garnish with cheese and serve warm.

Serving Suggestion: Serve the sloppy joe with some vegan cheese on top.

Variation Tip: Add cabbage coleslaw to the sloppy joe.

Nutritional Information Per Serving:

Calories 341 | Fat 24g |Sodium 547mg | Carbs 24g | Fiber 1.2g | Sugar 1g | Protein 10.3g

Sesame-Orange Chickpea Stir-Fry

Prep Time: 15 minutes.

Cook Time: 25 minutes.

Serves: 6

Ingredients:

Sauce:

- ¾ cup orange juice
- 1 tablespoon honey
- 2 tablespoons soy sauce
- 1 teaspoon ginger, grated
- 1 tablespoon cornstarch organic
- Zest of 1 orange

Stir-fry:

- 1½ tablespoon toasted sesame oil
- 1 (15-ounce) can chickpeas, rinsed
- ½ red onion, chopped
- 3 garlic cloves, minced
- 1 large red bell pepper, sliced
- 8 ounces green beans, chopped

- Green onion, for garnish
- Toasted sesame seeds, for garnish
- Red pepper flakes
- Cooked Quinoa, for serving

Preparation:

1. Mix orange zest, cornstarch, ginger, soy sauce, honey, and orange juice in a large bowl.
2. Set a suitable skillet with 1 tablespoon sesame oil over medium-high heat.
3. Stir in chickpeas then sauté for 5 minutes.
4. Mix well and transfer the chickpeas to a plate.
5. Sauté onion with ½ tablespoons oil in a skillet over medium heat for 4 minutes.
6. Stir in bell pepper and garlic then sauté for 3 minutes.
7. Add green beans then sauté for 4 minutes.
8. Pour in the prepared sauce then mix and cook until the sauce thickens.
9. Add chickpeas and cook on low heat for 4 minutes.
10. Garnish with green onion, red pepper flakes and sesame seeds.
11. Serve warm.

Serving Suggestion: Serve the stir-fry with zucchini noodles or rice.

Variation Tip: Add peas to the stir-fry.

Nutritional Information Per Serving:

Calories 318 | Fat 15.7g | Sodium 124mg | Carbs 31g | Fiber 0.1g | Sugar 0.3g | Protein 4.9g

Sweet Potato Zoodles

Prep Time: 15 minutes.

Cook Time: 21 minutes.

Serves: 4

Ingredients:

- 1 teaspoon coconut oil
- 3 garlic cloves, minced
- 2 teaspoons fresh grated ginger
- 1 small white onion, diced
- 1 red pepper, diced
- 2 medium sweet potatoes, peeled and diced
- 1¼ teaspoon ground turmeric
- ½ teaspoon salt
- Black pepper, to taste
- 1 (15-ounce) can light coconut milk
- 2 tablespoons creamy peanut butter
- 2 medium zucchinis, spiralized

Preparation:

1. Sauté ginger, and garlic with oil in a suitable skillet for 30 seconds.
2. Stir in sweet potatoes cubes, onion and red pepper then cook for 5 minutes.
3. Add turmeric, coconut milk, black pepper, salt and peanut butter then cook to a boil.
4. Reduce its heat, and cook for 15 minutes.
5. Add zucchini noodles then mix well.
6. Garnish with green onion, cilantro and lime juice.
7. Serve warm.

Serving Suggestion: Serve the zoodles with tofu stir fry.

Variation Tip: Add vegan cheese on top of the zoodles.

Nutritional Information Per Serving:

Calories 391 | Fat 2.2g |Sodium 276mg | Carbs 27g | Fiber 0.9g | Sugar 1.4g | Protein 8.8g

Butternut Squash Chickpea Stew

Prep Time: 15 minutes.

Cook Time: 21 minutes.

Serves: 6

Ingredients:

- 1 tablespoon olive oil
- 1 medium white onion, chopped
- 6 garlic cloves, minced
- 2 teaspoons cumin
- 1 teaspoon cinnamon
- 1 teaspoon ground turmeric
- ¼ teaspoon cayenne pepper
- 1 (28-ounce) can crushed tomatoes
- 2½ cups vegetable broth
- 1 (15-ounce) can chickpeas, rinsed
- 4 cups butternut squash, cubed
- 1 cup green lentils, rinsed
- ½ teaspoon salt
- Black pepper, to taste
- fresh juice of ½ lemon
- ⅓ cup cilantro, chopped
- Basil leaves, chopped

Preparation:

1. Sauté garlic and onion with oil in a suitable pot over medium high heat for 5 minutes.
2. Stir in cayenne, turmeric, cinnamon and cumin then sauté for 30 seconds.
3. Add black pepper, salt, lentils. Butternut squash, chickpeas, broth and tomatoes.
4. Cook to a boil, reduce its heat then cover and cook for 20 minutes.
5. Add basil, cilantro and lemon juice.
6. Serve warm.

Serving Suggestion: Serve the stew with roasted mushrooms.

Variation Tip: Add lemon zest on top for better taste.

Nutritional Information Per Serving:

Calories 324 | Fat 5g | Sodium 432mg | Carbs 31g | Fiber 0.3g | Sugar 1g | Protein 5.7g

Puerto Rican Rice and Beans

Prep Time: 15 minutes.

Cook Time: 1 hr. 7 minutes.

Serves: 4

Ingredients:

Beans:

- 1-pound dry pinto beans
- 8 cups water
- 2 bay leaves
- Sofrito for the beans:
- 2 teaspoons olive oil
- ½ cup yellow onion, diced
- ½ cup green bell pepper, diced
- ¼ cup cilantro, chopped
- 3 garlic cloves, minced
- 1 cup tomato sauce
- 3 teaspoons/2 packets sazon

Rice:

- 2 teaspoons olive oil
- ⅓ cup yellow onion, diced
- ⅓ cup green bell pepper, chopped
- ¼ cup cilantro, chopped
- 2 garlic cloves, minced
- ½ cup tomato sauce
- 3 teaspoons/2 packets sazon
- ⅛ teaspoon adobo
- 1 (15-ounce) can Pigeon peas
- 3 cups water
- 2 cups basmati white rice

Preparation:

1. Soak beans in 8 cups water in a bowl for 8 hours then drain.
2. Boil beans with water in a cooking pot for 2 minutes then reduce the heat and cook for 2 hours.
3. Drain the beans and keep them aside.
4. Sauté onion, garlic, cilantro, green pepper with oil in a suitable pan for 5 minutes.
5. Reduce the heat and add sazon and tomato sauce then cook for 3 minutes.
6. Stir in beans and cook for 30 minutes.
7. Meanwhile, make rice and sauté onion, garlic, cilantro, and green with oil in a suitable pan for 5 minutes.
8. Stir in adobo, sazon and tomato sauce then cook for 2 minutes.

9. Add rice and 3 cups water then cook for 30 minutes.
10. Serve the rice with the beans and garnish with cilantro and avocado.
11. Enjoy warm.

Serving Suggestion: Serve the rice with sautéed asparagus.

Variation Tip: Add crumbled tofu to the rice.

Nutritional Information Per Serving:
Calories 136 | Fat 20g | Sodium 249mg | Carbs 24g | Fiber 2g | Sugar 3g | Protein 4g

Curried Brown Rice with Tofu

Prep Time: 15 minutes.

Cook Time: 62 minutes.

Serves: 4

Ingredients:

Tofu
- 1 package extra firm tofu, cubed
- ½ tablespoon olive oil
- 1 teaspoon yellow curry powder
- ½ teaspoon coconut sugar
- ½ teaspoon garlic powder
- 1 pinch of cayenne pepper
- ¼ teaspoon salt
- Black pepper, to taste

Veggies
- ½ tablespoon olive oil
- 3 garlic cloves, minced
- 8 ounces baby bella mushrooms, sliced
- 1 white onion, diced
- 1 red bell pepper, diced
- 2 large carrots, sliced

Rice
- 2 cups jasmine brown rice
- 1 can (15-ounce) light coconut milk
- 2 cups water
- 1 cup frozen peas
- 1 tablespoon yellow curry powder
- ½ teaspoon ground turmeric
- ¾ teaspoon salt
- Black pepper, to taste

Garnish
- ½ cup fresh cilantro, chopped
- ½ cup dried cranberries

Preparation:

1. Mix all ingredients for tofu marinade in a bowl then add tofu.
2. Toss, cover and refrigerate for 24 hours.
3. Sauté tofu with oil in a suitable skillet for 6 minutes per side.

4. Sauté mushrooms, carrots, bell pepper, onion, and garlic with ½ tablespoon olive oil in another pan for 5 minutes.
5. Add brown rice, coconut milk and rest of the ingredients then cook for 45 minutes on a simmer.
6. Add tofu to the rice and serve warm.
7. Enjoy.

Serving Suggestion: Serve the rice with fresh herbs on top.

Variation Tip: Add a drizzle of red pepper flakes on top.

Nutritional Information Per Serving:
Calories 351 | Fat 19g |Sodium 412mg | Carbs 33g | Fiber 0.3g | Sugar 1g | Protein 13g

Chapter 8: Desserts Recipes

Cashew Oat Muffins

Prep Time: 15 minutes.

Cook Time: 22 minutes.

Serves: 6

Ingredients:

- 3 cups rolled oats
- ¾ cup raw cashews, chopped
- ¼ cup maple syrup
- ¼ cup sugar
- 1 teaspoon vanilla extract
- ½ teaspoon salt
- 1½ teaspoons baking soda
- 2 cups water

Preparation:

1. Preheat your oven to 375°F.
2. Grind the rolled oats in a food processor.
3. Separately, whisk together the dry ingredients in one bowl and the wet ingredients in another bowl.
4. Beat the two mixtures together until smooth.
5. Fold in cashews and give it a gentle stir.
6. Line a muffin tray with muffin cups and evenly divide the muffin batter among the cups.
7. Bake for 22 minutes and serve.

Serving Suggestion: Serve the muffins with a drizzle of coconut shred on top.

Variation Tip: Add a drizzle of applesauce on top.

Nutritional Information Per Serving:

Calories 261 | Fat 10g |Sodium 218mg | Carbs 26g | Fiber 10g | Sugar 30g | Protein 4g

Banana Walnut Muffins

Prep Time: 15 minutes.
Cook Time: 18 minutes.
Serves: 6

Ingredients:

- 4 large pitted dates, boiled
- 1 cup almond milk
- 2 tablespoons lemon juice
- 2½ cups rolled oats
- 1 teaspoon baking powder
- 1 teaspoon baking soda
- 1 teaspoon cinnamon
- ¼ teaspoon nutmeg
- ⅛ teaspoon salt
- 1½ cups mashed banana
- ¼ cup maple syrup
- 1 tablespoon vanilla extract
- 1 cup walnuts, chopped

Preparation:

1. Preheat your oven to 350°F .
2. Separately, whisk together the dry ingredients in one bowl and the wet ingredients in another bowl.
3. Beat the two mixtures together until smooth.
4. Fold in walnuts and give it a gentle stir.
5. Line a suitable muffin tray with muffin cups and evenly divide the muffin batter among the cups.
6. Bake for 18 minutes and serve.

Serving Suggestion: Serve the muffins with melted chocolate on top.

Variation Tip: Add chocolate chips to the muffins.

Nutritional Information Per Serving:

Calories 118 | Fat 20g |Sodium 192mg | Carbs 19g | Fiber 0.9g | Sugar 19g | Protein 5.2g

Protein Fat Bombs

Prep Time: 10 minutes.

Cook Time: 0 minutes.

Serves: 6

Ingredients:

- 1 cup coconut oil
- 1 cup peanut butter, melted
- ½ cup cocoa powder
- ¼ cup plant-based protein powder
- 1 pinch of salt
- 2 cups unsweetened coconut, shredded

Preparation:

1. Mix oil, peanut butter, cocoa powder, protein powder and salt in a suitable bowl.
2. Then make small balls out of this mixture and place them into silicone molds.
3. Freeze for 1 hour to set.
4. Roll the balls in the coconut shreds
5. Serve.

Serving Suggestion: Serve the fat bombs with a blueberry smoothie on the side.

Variation Tip: Add chopped nuts to the fat bombs.

Nutritional Information Per Serving:

Calories 248 | Fat 16g |Sodium 95mg | Carbs 34g | Fiber 0.3g | Sugar 10g | Protein 14.1g

Apple Pie Bites

Prep Time: 10 minutes.
Cook Time: 0 minutes.
Serves: 6

Ingredients:

- 1 cup walnuts, chopped
- ½ cup coconut oil
- ¼ cup ground flax seeds
- ½ ounce freeze-dried apples
- 1 teaspoon vanilla extract
- 1 teaspoon cinnamon
- Liquid stevia, to taste

Preparation:

1. In a bowl, add all the ingredients.
2. Mix well, then roll the mixture into small balls.
3. Freeze them for 1 hour to set.
4. Serve.

Serving Suggestion: Serve the pies with chocolate sauce on top.

Variation Tip: Add crushed pecans to the filling.

Nutritional Information Per Serving:

Calories 217 | Fat 12g |Sodium 79mg | Carbs 28g | Fiber 1.1g | Sugar 18g | Protein 5g

Peach Popsicles

Prep Time: 10 minutes.

Cook Time: 0 minutes.

Serves: 6

Ingredients:

- 2½ cups peaches, peeled and pitted
- 2 tablespoons agave
- ¾ cup coconut cream

Preparation:

1. Blend peaches with cream and agave in a blender until smooth.
2. Divide the popsicle blend into the popsicle molds.
3. Insert the popsicle sticks and close the molds.
4. Place these molds in the freezer for 2 hours to set.
5. Serve.

Serving Suggestion: Serve the popsicle with a drizzle of chocolate on top.

Variation Tip: Add crushed walnuts or pecans to the popsicles.

Nutritional Information Per Serving:

Calories 195 | Fat 3g | Sodium 355mg | Carbs 17g | Fiber 1g | Sugar 25g | Protein 1g

Green Popsicles

Prep Time: 10 minutes.

Cook Time: 0 minutes.

Serves: 4

Ingredients:

- 1 ripe avocado, peeled and pitted
- 1 cup fresh spinach
- 1 can (13.5-ounce) full fat coconut milk
- ¼ cup lime juice
- 2 tablespoons maple syrup
- 1 teaspoon vanilla extract

Preparation:

1. Blend vanilla, maple, lime juice, spinach, coconut milk and avocado in a blender until smooth.
2. Divide the popsicle blend into the popsicle molds.
3. Insert the popsicle sticks and close the molds.
4. Place these molds in the freezer for 2 hours to set.
5. Serve.

Serving Suggestion: Serve the popsicle with a drizzle of chocolate on top.

Variation Tip: Add crushed walnuts or pecans to the popsicles.

Nutritional Information Per Serving:

Calories 203 | Fat 8.9g | Sodium 340mg | Carbs 22g | Fiber 1.2g | Sugar 11.3g | Protein 5.3g

Strawberry Coconut Popsicles

Prep Time: 10 minutes.

Cook Time: 0 minutes.

Serves: 4

Ingredients:

- 2 medium bananas, sliced
- 1 can coconut milk
- 1 cup strawberries
- 3 tablespoons maple syrup

Preparation:

1. Blend coconut milk, maple, strawberries and bananas in a blender until smooth.
2. Divide the popsicle blend into the popsicle molds.
3. Insert the popsicle sticks and close the molds.
4. Place these molds in the freezer for 2 hours to set.
5. Serve.

Serving Suggestion: Serve the popsicles with chocolate syrup on top.

Variation Tip: Add crushed cashews to the popsicles.

Nutritional Information Per Serving:

Calories 153 | Fat 1g | Sodium 8mg | Carbs 16g | Fiber 0.8g | Sugar 56g | Protein 1g

Crunchy Chocolate Brownies

Prep Time: 1 hour 15 minutes.

Cook Time: 1 minute.

Serves: 4

Ingredients:

Filling

- 2 cups dates, pitted
- 2 cups walnuts
- Pinch of sea salt
- 2 tablespoons water

Topping

- 1 dark chocolate bar, chopped
- ½ cup peanut butter
- 1 tablespoon coconut oil

Preparation:

1. Add pitted dates to water in a bowl and soak for 10 minutes, then drain.
2. Add walnuts to a blender and pulse until it forms a crumble.
3. Stir sea, salt, cacao powder, dates, and 1 tablespoon water to the blender.
4. Blend again until it forms a thick date dough.
5. Spread this mixture in an 8-inch baking pan lined with a parchment sheet.
6. Press the dough in the pan, then freeze for 1 hour.
7. Meanwhile, melt peanut butter, coconut oil, and chocolate chips in a glass bowl by heating in the microwave.
8. Pour this chocolate melt over the dates batter.
9. Allow it to sit, then slice.
10. Serve.

Serving Suggestion: Serve the brownies with keto chocolate syrup on top.

Variation Tip: Add crushed walnuts or pecans to the brownies.

Nutritional Information Per Serving:

Calories 198 | Fat 14g | Sodium 272mg | Carbs 17g | Fiber 1g | Sugar 9.3g | Protein 1.3g

Chickpea Meringues

Prep Time: 10 minutes.

Cook Time: 2 hours.

Serves: 6

Ingredients:

- 1 (15-ounce) can chickpeas
- ¼ teaspoon cream of tartar
- Kosher salt
- ¾ cup of sugar

Preparation:

1. Layer 2 baking sheets with parchment sheet and preheat the oven to 250°F.
2. Drain the chickpeas and reserve ¾ cup of its liquid.
3. Blend the chickpeas with cream of tartar, a pinch of salt, and the reserved liquid in the blender.
4. Add this mixture to a piping bag and pipe the mixture drop by drop on the baking sheet.
5. Bake these meringue drops for 2 hours in the preheated oven until firm.
6. Cool and serve.

Serving Suggestion: Serve the meringue with vegan cookies.

Variation Tip: Dip the meringue in melted chocolate.

Nutritional Information Per Serving:

Calories 159 | Fat 3g | Sodium 277mg | Carbs 39g | Fiber 1g | Sugar 9g | Protein 2g

Watermelon Coconut Sorbet

Prep Time: 15 minutes.

Cook Time: 0 minutes.

Serves: 6

Ingredients:

- 5 cups seedless watermelon, peeled and diced
- 4 cups coconut milk
- ¼ cup coconut syrup
- Juice from ½ lemon

Preparation:

1. Blend watermelon with the rest of the ingredients in a blender until smooth.
2. Spread this mixture in a baking dish and cover it with plastic wrap.
3. Freeze the watermelon mixture for 4 hours.
4. Cut the frozen mixture into cubes and blend in a food processor.
5. Spread this mixture in the baking dish and freeze again for 2 hours.
6. Scoop out and serve.

Serving Suggestion: Serve the sorbet with a glass of green smoothie.

Variation Tip: Add crushed berries on top of the sorbet.

Nutritional Information Per Serving:

Calories 245 | Fat 14g |Sodium 122mg | Carbs 28g | Fiber 1.2g | Sugar 12g | Protein 4.3g

Chapter 9: 30-Day Meal Plan

Week 1

Day 1:

Breakfast: Pumpkin Oatmeal

Lunch: Coconut Green Soup

Snack: Zucchini Chips

Dinner: Sesame-Orange Chickpea Stir-Fry

Dessert: Cashew Oat Muffins

Day 2:

Breakfast: Cauliflower Oatmeal

Lunch: Roasted Cauliflower Soup

Snack: Carrot Chips

Dinner: Lentil Sloppy Joes with Spaghetti Squash

Dessert: Banana Walnut Muffins

Day 3:

Breakfast: Berry Cobbler

Lunch: Squash and Chestnut Soup

Snack: Kale Chips

Dinner: Pineapple Tofu Kabobs

Dessert: Protein Fat Bombs

Day 4:

Breakfast: Protein Bars

Lunch: Shiitake Tortilla Soup

Snack: Roasted Chickpeas

Dinner: Black Bean Loaf with Avocado Sauce

Dessert: Apple Pie Bites

Day 5:

Breakfast: Hemp Breakfast Cookies

Lunch: Vegan Tomato Soup

Snack: Spicy Almonds

Dinner: Vegetarian Lentil Loaf

Dessert: Peach Popsicles

Day 6:

Breakfast: Strawberry Coconut Chia Pudding

Lunch: Pita Pizzas

Snack: Seeds Crackers

Dinner: Taco Pasta with Sweet Corn

Dessert: Green Popsicles

Day 7:

Breakfast: Zucchini Oatmeal

Lunch: Black Bean Burgers

Snack: Apple Leather

Dinner: Cashew Mac and Cheese

Dessert: Crunchy Chocolate Brownies

Week 2

Day 1:

Breakfast: Peanut Butter Muffins

Lunch: Spinach-Potato Tacos

Snack: Banana Chips

Dinner: Roasted Butternut Squash Pasta

Dessert: Chickpea Meringues

Day 2:

Breakfast: Peanut Butter Muffins

Lunch: Sweet Potato Quesadillas

Snack: Zucchini Chips

Dinner: Sweet Potato Penne Pasta

Dessert: Watermelon Coconut Sorbet

Day 3:

Breakfast: Chocolate Zucchini Bread

Lunch: Slow-Cooker Chili

Snack: Carrot Chips

Dinner: Butternut Squash Lasagna

Dessert: Green Popsicles

Day 4:

Breakfast: Corn Muffins

Lunch: Sweet Potato Chili with Kale

Snack: Kale Chips

Dinner: Lime Bean Artichoke Wraps

Dessert: Cashew Oat Muffins

Day 5:

Breakfast: Pumpkin Oatmeal

Lunch: Potato-Cauliflower Curry

Snack: Roasted Chickpeas

Dinner: Avocado Chickpea Lettuce Cups

Dessert: Banana Walnut Muffins

Day 6:

Breakfast: Cauliflower Oatmeal

Lunch: Zucchini and Chickpea Sauté

Snack: Spicy Almonds

Dinner: Curried Brown Rice with Tofu

Dessert: Protein Fat Bombs

Day 7:

Breakfast: Cauliflower Oatmeal

Lunch: Raw Collard Wraps

Snack: Seeds Crackers

Dinner: Puerto Rican Rice and Beans

Dessert: Apple Pie Bites

Week 3

Day 1:

Breakfast: Berry Cobbler

Lunch: Avocado Chickpea Lettuce Cups

Snack: Apple Leather

Dinner: Butternut Squash Chickpea Stew

Dessert: Peach Popsicles

Day 2:

Breakfast: Protein Bars

Lunch: Coconut Green Soup

Snack: Banana Chips

Dinner: Sweet Potato Zoodles

Dessert: Green Popsicles

Day 3:

Breakfast: Hemp Breakfast Cookies

Lunch: Roasted Cauliflower Soup

Snack: Zucchini Chips

Dinner: Sesame-Orange Chickpea Stir-Fry

Dessert: Strawberry Coconut Popsicles

Day 4:

Breakfast: Strawberry Coconut Chia Pudding

Lunch: Squash and Chestnut Soup

Snack: Carrot Chips

Dinner: Lentil Sloppy Joes with Spaghetti Squash

Dessert: Crunchy Chocolate Brownies

Day 5:

Breakfast: Zucchini Oatmeal

Lunch: Shiitake Tortilla Soup

Snack: Kale Chips

Dinner: Pineapple Tofu Kabobs

Dessert: Chickpea Meringues

Day 6:

Breakfast: Peanut Butter Muffins

Lunch: Vegan Tomato Soup

Snack: Roasted Chickpeas

Dinner: Black Bean Loaf with Avocado Sauce

Dessert: Watermelon Coconut Sorbet

Day 7:

Breakfast: Chocolate Zucchini Bread

Lunch: Black Bean Burgers

Snack: Spicy Almonds

Dinner: Vegetarian Lentil Loaf

Dessert: Cashew Oat Muffins

Week 4

Day 1:
Breakfast: Corn Muffins

Lunch: Spinach-Potato Tacos

Snack: Apple Leather

Dinner: Taco Pasta with Sweet Corn

Dessert: Banana Walnut Muffins

Day 2:
Breakfast: Pumpkin Oatmeal

Lunch: Sweet Potato Quesadillas

Snack: Banana Chips

Dinner: Cashew Mac and Cheese

Dessert: Protein Fat Bombs

Day 3:
Breakfast: Cauliflower Oatmeal

Lunch: Slow-Cooker Chili

Snack: Zucchini Chips

Dinner: Roasted Butternut Squash Pasta

Dessert: Apple Pie Bites

Day 4:
Breakfast: Berry Cobbler

Lunch: Sweet Potato Chili with Kale

Snack: Carrot Chips

Dinner: Sweet Potato Penne Pasta

Dessert: Peach Popsicles

Day 5:
Breakfast: Protein Bars

Lunch: Potato-Cauliflower Curry

Snack: Kale Chips

Dinner: Butternut Squash Lasagna

Dessert: Green Popsicles

Day 6:
Breakfast: Hemp Breakfast Cookies

Lunch: Zucchini and Chickpea Sauté

Snack: Roasted Chickpeas

Dinner: Sweet Potato Penne Pasta

Dessert: Strawberry Coconut Popsicles

Day 7:
Breakfast: Strawberry Coconut Chia Pudding

Lunch: Raw Collard Wraps

Snack: Spicy Almonds

Dinner: Lime Bean Artichoke Wraps

Dessert: Crunchy Chocolate Brownies

Conclusion

Perhaps, you can too, enjoy the claimed benefits of a plant-based diet with all the wide-ranging delicious recipes shared in this cookbook. The plant-based diet is often regarded as an umbrella term for all the different approaches used to consumed plant-sourced food on a diet. The proponents of this diet see plant-sourced food as a source of lots of clean energy and nutrients. Plant are reservoirs of both macro- and micronutrients that meet all the human body's needs. So, when you are eating plant-sourced food, you are adding a lot of added minerals, vitamins, and phytonutrients, which improves metabolism and other bodily functions. This diet is also widely popular because it helps reduce the intake of animal-sourced products from meat to dairy and other processed food. Some people value this diet for its health benefits, whereas others for its animal-friendly approach. You can have all the ingredients marked and follow the weekly plant-based meal plan from this book. This cookbook only come as a guideline for those who are looking for new ways to go vegan with ease.

© Copyright 2021 - All rights reserved.

The content contained within this book may not be reproduced, duplicated or transmitted without direct written permission from the author or the publisher.

Under no circumstances will any blame or legal responsibility be held against the publisher, or author, for any damages, reparation, or monetary loss due to the information contained within this book, either directly or indirectly.

Legal Notice:

This book is copyright protected. It is only for personal use. You cannot amend, distribute, sell, use, quote or paraphrase any part, or the content within this book, without the consent of the author or publisher.

Disclaimer Notice:

Please note the information contained within this document is for educational and entertainment purposes only. All effort has been executed to present accurate, up to date, reliable, complete information. No warranties of any kind are declared or implied. Readers acknowledge that the author is not engaged in the rendering of legal, financial, medical or professional advice. The content within this book has been derived from various sources. Please consult a licensed professional before attempting any techniques outlined in this book.

By reading this document, the reader agrees that under no circumstances is the author responsible for any losses, direct or indirect, that are incurred as a result of the use of the information contained within this document, including, but not limited to, errors, omissions, or inaccuracies.